God's BIG plan for the world

Paul Godfrey

Scripture
Union

Suggested timing

The core programme is divided into group times **G** and all together times **A**

G	Welcome	**20 minutes**

On line in the Upload Zone

A	Sing	**5 minutes**
A	Pogo Challenge	**8 minutes**
A	Video	**10 minutes**
A	Soundbyte	**7 minutes**
A	Interactivity	**10 minutes**
G	Activity Sheet	**10 minutes**
G	Refreshments	**5 minutes**
A **G**	Games	**20 minutes**
G	Craft	**30 minutes**

Back in the Upload Zone

A	*The Virus Buster* Drama	**10 minutes**
A	Songs and goodbye	**15 minutes**

Post it

Most people like a programme that is easy to use. But the numbers, venue, timing and unique features of your holiday club mean that you must tailor the programme to your needs.

The suggested programme for each day is only one way of running **MegaQuest.** It is timed for two and a half hours. Precise times have not been given.

For Caroline, Hannah, Andrew and Richard with love.

Thanks to the teams at Christ Church Bedford, Houghton Regis Baptist and the Stables, Bourn.

© Paul Godfrey 1998

First published 1998

ISBN 1 85999 284 6

Scripture Union, 207-209 Queensway, Bletchley, Milton Keynes, MK2 2EB

The artwork, activity sheets, scripts and music in this publication may be photocopied for use in running the MegaQuest holiday club programme, without reference to current copyright legislation or any copyright licensing scheme. Outside this provision, no part of this publication may be reproduced, stored in a retrieval system or transmitted, in any form or by any means, electronic or mechanical, by photocopying, recording or otherwise, without prior permission of Scripture Union. All rights reserved.

The right of Paul Godfrey to be identified as author of this work has been asserted by him in acordance with the Copyright, Designs and Patents Act 1988.

British Library Cataloguing-in-Publication Data

A catalogue record for this book is available from the British Library.

Scripture quotations are from the CEV © British & Foreign Bible Society 1996

Design by Heather Knight, Grax Design Consultants

Illustrations by Helen Gale, Colin Smithson

Cover illustration by Colin Smithson

Printed and bound in Great Britain by Ebenezer Baylis & Son Ltd, The Trinity Press, London Road, Worcester, WR5 2JH

Contents

Why run a MegaQuest week 4

Introducing MegaQuest 5

Putting MegaQuest into practice 6

Stay legal! 7

Confidential declaration 8

Planning checklist 9

Sample invitation and registration form 10

Publicity, further information and consent form 11

Training the team 12

MegaQuest song 13

Getting your venue ready 14

Practical stuff - using an OHP, computer and video 16

Words of song 17

Day 1 artwork for craft activity 18

Day 3 artwork for craft activity 19

Day 5 artwork for craft activity 20

Extra artwork 21

Pogo challenge 22

Drama script - *The Virus Buster* 23

Day 1 - The garden 32

Day 2 - The mountain 38

Day 3 - The hill 44

Day 4 - The road 50

Day 5 - The city 56

After MegaQuest 62

What's on the MegaQuest website? 63

Resources order form 64

Why run a MegaQuest week?

No one but the leaders of your holiday club can identify your aims and there isn't space in a resource book like this to outline all the issues that need to be part of your thinking, planning and praying. However, here are a few pointers. For more help read *Nuts and Bolts*, the Scripture Union guide to running holiday clubs, term-time missions and other special events (see inside front cover for details).

1

Is the club part of the church's overall outreach activities?

If you only plan the holiday club for the children you already see regularly, you will be missing out on a valuable evangelistic opportunity. At least 85% of the children who live round you are unlikely to be in touch with any church. But if you do your praying, planning and publicity even half right, a good number of them will come to a special club week.

Special events are excellent, but they are far more effective if they are part of a larger strategy which includes outreach, nurture and keeping-in-touch activities for all ages.

2

Do you have a vision to reach families, rather than just children?

Children who go home enthusiastic about all that's going on at a holiday club are a powerful means to warm otherwise cold contacts. So use the warmth before it cools! Plan at least one invitation event for those of all ages who live with or relate closely to the children - grandparents, child-minders, older and younger brothers and sisters and so on - not just parents. How will you nurture those contacts afterwards? Begin to plan now.

3

Have you thought through the timing and venue of your club?

Timing	Advantages	Disadvantages
School holidays	Use the free time that children have. Offer something to stave off boredom. Get children outside in the fresh air (but don't count on it!).	Some potential team leaders, or those children you hope will come, may be away. The team needs to be out of paid work, work shifts, or be willing and able to take time off. Term-times (using a slot between school and bed, ie 3.30-5, or 6-7.30).
Term-times	You can utilise team members who are in full-time employment. It's easier to advertise the club, ie through school. Word goes around the school from satisfied customers. Children and leaders are not likely to be away.	Children may have regular after-school activities. Children (especially younger ones) may be tired.

Venue

A community hall or a school is neutral territory for unchurched children and their parents. Schools are also usually better equipped and ought to be child-friendly and familiar. However, you may want children and parents to come onto church premises through a child-friendly, unthreatening activity and hiring non-church premises can be costly.

4

What do you hope will happen after the club?

Plan events to keep in touch with contacts you make. If you want to encourage children to join your regular activities, make sure that the leaders of these activities are around during the club week. A non-Sunday club is usually the best way to keep in regular contact. It doesn't need to be weekly if that would be too much for you to resource. A monthly event is a great deal better than nothing.

God's BIG plan for the world

Introducing MegaQuest

MegaQuest teaches the shape of God's plan of salvation through the theme of a computer game. Each day a stage in God's plan is mirrored by the next level of the game. The theme is carried into some of the activities, but there is no need for you to be computer-literate. There are, however, a number of suggestions for those with access to computer hardware on page 16.

Before you assume this doesn't include you, think about those in your church, or on the fringes, who may use a computer at work or at home. They may have ideas of their own! Extra ideas are on the SU website on page 63.

Trying to cover God's BIG plan in a week means a big picture approach rather than a detailed one. It's ambitious but possible as you will discover.

1   Level 1: **The garden** (Genesis 1,2; Hebrews 1:3; 1 Peter 1:20)

God makes all that there is and puts his print on it. In particular he makes people in his own image. His creation is very good. God doesn't make mistakes. But straight away, sin spoils the relationship with God, spoils the world and distorts God's image in people. Thankfully, nothing surprises God and he already has a plan, for one day someone will live a life of which, from beginning to end, God will be able to say, 'I am well pleased'.

2   Level 2: **The mountain** (Exodus 19,20; Galatians 3:15–25)

God wants people to know how they should live in his world. He chooses a people and gives them his law. Despite their words of commitment, the law is broken almost from the moment it is given. But God has a plan: one day someone will live a perfect life – God's way – in God's world.

3   Level 3: **The hill** (Matthew 27; Mark 15; Luke 23; John 19; Romans 5:1–11)

God himself enters his world in Jesus who lives the perfect life, shows God's love and dies as the remedy for sin. It looks like a horrible mistake, but nothing surprises God. This is the crux of God's plan and there is more to come...

4   Level 4: **The road** (Luke 24:13-35)

The resurrection completes the central event of salvation, but the truth dawns slowly even on the disciples. Nothing surprises God, but he surprises people. For example, two of Jesus' disciples find out the truth about Jesus on an evening walk and over a meal. Now, having gone to heaven, he is available to people of all ages by his Spirit. He calls them to know him personally and will help them to change how they live.

5   Level 5: **The city** (Revelation 21,22)

Heaven! No more death, no more crying, the river of life, the golden city. 'The term is over: the holidays have begun. The dream has ended: this is the morning.' (CS Lewis *The Last Battle*)

Putting MegaQuest into practice

The six components of **MegaQuest** include both small group and all together times. The two should complement each other. Building relationships and talking together in small groups is the time when children can see the reality of a relationship with Jesus and all that **MegaQuest** means. This is the heart of a good holiday club.

The core programme is divided into group times **G** and all together times **A**

1 **A G** The welcome

Over the week, each group should attempt to build a model computer from the junk you've supplied. This helps to make children feel welcome, and builds relationships. It is important that a group starts with the screen, as once it is made, it can be used to display a picture relating to each day's theme. This acts as a reminder and possible conversation starter on subsequent days. You can use (and enlarge) the colouring picture on each day's activity sheet or the picture at the head of each day.

Children could make a printer, keyboard and mouse. Add batteries, bulbs and a buzzer and see who can build a simple circuit to add to the effect.

2 **A G** The teaching input

Use the **MegaQuest** video and the talk outline (Soundbyte), or just Soundbyte on its own. Songs and suggested group-based interactive games, called Interactivities, help to reinforce the content.

This can be followed by discussions in small groups, using the activity sheets given for each day's programme. There are puzzles for older and younger children. You may want to adapt the sheet for your needs. In this book, each activity sheet can be folded into an A5 leaflet. While the children use the activity sheet, continue to talk with individuals. If time is tight, you could follow up the discussion with the themed crafts included in each day's programme and use the sheet as a take-home extra. Alternatively, the activity sheet could be used in the next day's programme to act as a reminder of what has happened before.

3 **G** Crafts

There are suggested craft activities which relate to each day's theme and provide more opportunity to talk about the Bible themes. If you choose alternative

craft activities make sure at least one person on your team feels comfortable and competent to lead. For example, for older children one option linked to the computer theme is to create an electronics project. On Day 3, you'll find a wiring diagram for a quiz machine. This is intended for use as a large quiz accessory and could be reused in other contexts, but it would also work as a project built into a small box. If you can get enough computers together and a colour printer, you could have a group working on computer-generated pictures. The inside front cover gives details of resource books.

4 **G** Drama: *The Virus Buster*

Drama encourages involvement, continuity and therefore regular attendance to see what happens next. In *The Virus Buster*, the Programmer has written the perfect game. Characters have unlimited freedom to enjoy almost all levels of the computer game - only one area is forbidden. But there are baddies around, with a virus which will ruin everything. Without too many rehearsals and with a few costumes and props, the drama reinforces the basic outline of God's BIG plan for salvation.

5 **A** The Upload Zone

The look, sound and feel of your venue can be made to reflect the theme of that day's level, using decoration, lighting, projection, sound effects, even smells. Each day should be different. On page 4 you will find a range of suggestions for changing all or part of the space you use each day. These are expanded on the web site. Think imaginatively and creatively about how you can use these ideas to draw the children into the theme and reinforce the memorability of the whole experience.

6 **A** Plenty of fun

Find time for really good games which are full of fun, even if it's only 10 minutes in the middle of the session. Try to get some equipment which is different from what you might use at a regular club, for example, a tug-of-war rope, earthball, parachute or bouncy castle. These are often available from play or denominational resource centres. The Pogo Challenge on page 22 imitates the bouncing antics of a typical platform game hero. It can be fitted more than once into each programme.

Stay Legal!

The welfare of the children we hope to reach through **MegaQuest** is of paramount importance. We are concerned for their spiritual welfare, but also of course for their physical and emotional welfare. Sadly nowadays, children are at risk as much as ever before, and it is our duty to do all we can to ensure their safety and well-being as we aim to show them God's love.

As good practice, all team members should be made aware of the current legislation arising from the Children Act 1989 as it affects this kind of activity. The issues that affect **MegaQuest** are to do with daycare of children, especially relating to children under eight years old. But they are appropriate for all children attending a church-run event. The following guidelines must be taken into consideration during your initial planning:

- You may need to register **MegaQuest** with Social Services if you use your premises for more than two hours in a day. Even if you choose to run a programme longer than two hours (but less than four in a day) you have up to six exemption days a year, so one five-day holiday club will not be required to register but you should in any case inform Social Services in writing of your plans. Any holiday club over two hours which runs for more than six days in a year must be registered. So if you are planning follow-up events, it might affect you. If in doubt phone Social Services and check with the Local Day Care Advisor – he or she is there to help!

Even if you don't need to register, give careful consideration to the following requirements laid down by the Children Act, as sensible guidelines to be interpreted with commonsense. If you must register you won't have any choice!

- Requirements for accommodation state that the premises should be warm and adequately lit and ventilated.

- Minimum unencumbered floor space to be provided for children aged 5–8 years is 25 square feet (2.3 square metres) per child. In other words, be careful about very large numbers of children in a small hall and work out the maximum number of children who can attend.

- The premises you use should meet the Health and Safety requirements. Check that the owners of the premises have complied with all the requirements. Ideally there should be one toilet and one handbasin for every ten children.

- If you are preparing food on site, you will need to be inspected by the Environmental Health Office. Ideally, any sandwiches should be refrigerated (for example, if the children bring packed lunches). Smoking should not be permitted on the premises.

- Any accidents or incidents occurring during a session must be recorded in an Accident Book. This is essential in the event of any insurance claim. A record of the matter should be noted, along with details of the action taken. It should be countersigned where appropriate.

- Everyone should be made aware of emergency procedures and fire exits, and there must be access to a telephone. This could be a mobile phone, if necessary. A first-aid kit must be easily accessible and at least one member of your team should have a working knowledge of first aid.

- All groups need liability insurance. Make sure your activity is adequately covered by your church's policy.

- Recommendations for adult to child ratios are as follows:

  For 0–2 years – 1 adult to every 3 children (1:3)

  For 2–3 years – 1 adult to every 4 children (1:4)

  For 3–8 years – 1 adult to every 8 children (1:8)

  For over eights – 1 adult for the first 8 children, followed by 1 for every 12 (1:12).

  There should always be more than one adult for any group and one should be female.

- Let your team members know that it is not appropriate for them to talk to children alone in a secluded place – it might be misinterpreted.

- Do not allow people not known to you to have unsupervised access to the children. Sadly, touching children is not advisable now, although the government has recently made it clear that such actions as guiding with a hand on the shoulder or comforting a distressed young child would not be considered inappropriate. It is a question of common sense in this area, but if in doubt, don't!

- You must have an agreed procedure in the case of a child disclosing abuse or a situation which puts them at risk.

Confidential declaration form for potential members

Most denominations now have established good practice policies. All churches, whether denominational or not should have clear child protection policies. Where such good practice is ignored insurance may be invalid. If you have an established procedure for your church, all of the holiday club team must go through the process. If you haven't yet, a special club week may well be a good opportunity to establish one. The following notes outline the main issues.

All employed people with access to children (that is, anyone under the age of eighteen) have, by law, to make a signed declaration of any criminal record. A key recommendation in *Safe from Harm* (HMSO) also requires such a statement from volunteers. Failure to take the necessary steps could lead to a claim of negligence against the church if a child comes to any harm at the hand of anyone working with them in a voluntary capacity. 'Harm' includes ill-treatment of any kind (including sexual abuse), or impairment of physical or mental health or development.

- You should ask all potential team members to sign a form such as the one below.

- When using such a form, emphasise that it represents positive action for good practice, and slur or suspicion is not implied. Obviously the nature of the form is sensitive and should be handled with care.

- Ensure that confidentiality is maintained. In accordance with the Data Protection Act, do not divulge any information to third parties.

- If anyone gives a 'yes' answer, allow the individual to explain this disclosure personally or by letter. If you are in any doubt about the person's suitability, consult your church leader.

- As well as the declaration form, it is recommended that potential team members offer one name as a referee. Questions to ask a referee might include:

  - In what capacity have you known the applicant, and for how long?

  - How willing and able is he/she to work with others?

  - How suitable would you consider him/her for work with children and young people?

  - Are there any relevant details about this applicant which cause you concern?

CONFIDENTIAL DECLARATION

Guidelines from the Home Office following the Children Act 1989 advise that all voluntary organisations, including churches, take steps to safeguard the children who are entrusted to their care. You are therefore asked to make the following declaration:

Have you ever been convicted of a criminal offence including any 'spent convictions' under the Rehabilitation of Offenders Act 1974 or been cautioned by the police or bound over to keep the peace?

Yes ☐

No ☐

Have you ever been held liable by a court for a civil wrong, or had an order made against you by a matrimonial or a family court?

Yes ☐

No ☐

Has your conduct ever caused, or been likely to cause harm to a child or put a child at risk, or, to your knowledge, has it ever been alleged that your conduct has resulted in any of these things?

Yes ☐

No ☐

Signed _____

Date _____

Because of the nature of the work for which you are applying, this post is exempt from the provision of Section 4(ii) of the Rehabilitation of Offenders Act 1974, by virtue of the Rehabilitation of Offenders Act 1974 (Exemptions) Order 1975, and you are therefore not entitled to withhold information about convictions which, for other purposes are 'spent' under the provisions of the Act. In the event of an appointment, any failure to disclose such convictions could result in the withdrawal of approval to work with children in the church.

A checklist for those considering a clubweek

Adjust this for your own situation

Six months to go:

1 Pray for guidance.
2 Decide on objectives for holding an event.
3 Agree length (number of days and length of sessions), date and time (bearing in mind local events etc).
4 Agree target age range, and how to split into smaller groups.
5 Agree and book venue.
6 Assess likely cost and agree budget.
7 Agree whether to invite an outside leader.
8 Look at available resources/theme packs and agree on a theme.
9 Agree on additional family event(s) - What? When? Where?
10 Assess number of leaders/helpers needed.

Four months to go:

1 Recruit helpers and consider their training needs.
2 Assess what computer expertise is needed. Visit the SU website.
3 Arrange for at least one training session.
4 Plan for a special family service to close the holiday club (including refreshments if possible).
5 Consider the possibility of doing school assemblies and other promotion in local schools
6 Check whether the Children's Act requires you to register the event.
7 Check insurance cover of the premises.

Three months to go:

1 Plan publicity, ie posters, local magazine/newsletter, leaflets.

Who does what?

One of the real spin-off benefits of a club week is the opportunity for church members to work together and for the gifts of different people to be recognised and used. The ideal team will have a balance of ages and both sexes. Work hard to ensure that there are men on the team to counter the widely-held prejudice that God is for women and children! If you use the whole programme you will need the following roles to be performed:

2 Organise a simple registration system.
3 Organise start/finish procedure for each session (make it parent-friendly and safe).

Two months to go:

1 Plan and organise the layout for the main session.
2 Begin the collection of materials you will need – especially ice cream tubs for day 2, divided yoghurt pots for day 3 and junk for the computer construction.
3 Run the first training event for helpers.
4 Distribute application forms and publicity.

One month to go:

1 Organise refreshments.
2 Organise activity sheets and materials.
3 Organise craft materials/equipment.
4 Organise games materials/equipment/the Interactivities.
5 Set in motion the organisation of the follow-up events.
6 Begin drama rehearsals.
7 Run second training event to ensure familiarity with the programme.

One week to go:

1 Hold the final briefing for everyone involved.
2 Drama rehearsals.
3 Music practice.
4 Prepare the venue and everything that is needed.
5 Pray and get others to pray before and during the events.

WANTED!
Pray-ers
Publicity and public relations 'experts'
Stage hands and artists (to create and set up the scenery in the Upload Zone)
Trainers to prepare the team members
Registration organisers
Group leaders
Group helpers
Actors (and someone to 'direct')
Musician(s)
Sound and lighting 'technicians'
Up-front leader(s)
Games organiser(s)
Refreshment providers
Time controller
Follow-up co-ordinators
Dismantlers (to tidy up at the end)
(Obviously some of these roles can be done by the same person/people, ie the registration organisers could also provide refreshments, and so on.)

Sample registration form and letter

Church address and date

Dear Parent/Guardian

MegaQuest is the holiday club organised by *(your church)* to be held *(date/times)* at *(venue)*. This is for any child aged *(state age range and/or school year)*. In **MegaQuest** we will be entering various levels of a computer game, having fun through games, craft and drama and discovering how we can attack a deadly virus! At the same time we will be discovering God's BIG plan for the world.

Your child would be very welcome to come, but because places are limited, you will need to book in advance. Places will be allocated on a first-come-first-served basis. The week is completely free of charge *(or state what are the charges and what they cover, such as refreshments or hire of the hall)*.

Please complete the form below and return it to *(give details)*. If you have any queries, please contact *(name)* on *(phone number)*. We are looking forward to seeing your child at **MegaQuest**.

Your name
MegaQuest co-ordinator

Registration form for **MegaQuest**. *(Allow plenty of space for details!)*

Please tear along the dotted line and return to ....
(One form per child please)

Full name of child .... M/F   Date of birth ....

Address ....

....

Telephone number ....

School .... Age on first day ....

Signature and name of parent/guardian ....

Name ....

Contact phone number during **MegaQuest** ....

Publicising MegaQuest

Consider who you are trying to reach:

- churched children.
- children who always come annually to a holiday club.
- children (and parents) who use your buildings for some other activity.
- children who are friends with those who already come.
- unchurched children with no current church links.

All these can be reached by invitations through their friends or the leaders. Posters around your premises will act as reminders.

But the key place to reach new children is at their school. There are all sorts of good reasons to build a good relationship with your local schools. Don't convey the idea that you are using the school as a direct mailing service for your publicity. Most schools will be willing to pass on a clear informative leaflet to parents, and many will allow a visit during assembly.

Few will arrive at a holiday club just because of a poster, but they are invaluable as memory joggers.

Think carefully about where best to put them. Where do people in your area hang about? That's when most people will read anything and everything rather than just walk by – for example, the school gate, bus-stop, health centre, local pub.

It can be very helpful to combine a publicity flyer with a registration form, so that people can register in advance. This not only saves the horrific queues that can happen on Day One, but also enables you to plan responsibly if the uptake exceeds your expectations. Many schools are willing to have a returns box for you to come back and collect later. This saves parents having to post or deliver forms.

Finally, cultivate contacts in the local media. Advance publicity is helpful, but rare. A photo and article during or after the week will raise the profile of your church, and be pre-publicity for whatever comes next!

Don't neglect publicity during the week, for example for your family event. If you use the activity sheets as take-home sheets, you could adapt them to include invitations and information to parents and carers.

Further information and consent form

Once a child has registered for **MegaQuest** more information needs to be returned to the co-ordinator and kept at the venue. It should include the following:

Name, address, phone number and age of the child

Emergency contact telephone number

GP's name and telephone number

Details of any known conditions or allergies

Name of the person collecting the child at the end of **MegaQuest**

In the unlikely event of illness or accident I give permission for any necessary medical treatment to be given by the nominated first aider. In an emergency and if I am not contactable, I am willing for my son/daughter to receive hospital treatment, including an anaesthetic. I understand that every effort will be made to contact me as soon as possible.

I confirm that the above details are correct to the best of my knowledge.

Signed (parent/guardian) _____ Date _____

Training the team

Once you have a group of people willing to join in **MegaQuest** you need to build them into a team. Whether they have responded to an appeal for help, or you have approached them individually, they need training for the task.

A local Scripture Union evangelist or associate may be able to help with this.

Ideally, you need at least two compulsory team training sessions – perhaps one evening meeting, followed by a day for prayer and preparation. Aim to cover the following:

- Team building (for instance, an activity or shared meal)

- Bible focus and prayer, looking at the aims and objectives

- Guidelines for building relationships with the children (see Dos and don'ts below)

- A look at the programme, including a run-through of the first day (p 32)

- Allocation of roles and responsibilities (p 9)

- Organising the practicalities

- Learning the theme song and others so that children find it easy to join in (p 13)

- Explaining Christian truth to children including any booklets you may wish to have available.

- Praying with children

- Discipline (see Dos and don'ts below)

- Safety and emergency policy

- Specific prayer for the event and the children

- Follow-up strategy (p62)

(A set of useful case studies for thinking about many of these issues is available on the **MegaQuest** web-site).

Dos and don'ts for group leaders and helpers:

Do direct the children's attention to what is going on at the front.

Don't forget the children's names. Learn them and use them.

Do encourage children to join in and make sure you join in with everything too.

Don't forget the quiet or shy children. Be on the look-out for them and sit with them.

Do split up disruptive or restless children and sit with, or between them, if necessary.

Don't leave the group alone unless really necessary.

Do make sure that only one person talks at a time – perhaps when they are holding a particular object

Don't hang around the edge of the room, chatting – there is time for that afterwards. Sitting with children during the together times is the best way to do many of the above.

Do pray for the children.

Using Songs

Songs are an important part of a holiday club. They offer a means of tucking truth into memories. Most children love singing but some hate it, so don't overdo it.

The theme song is designed to mirror the shape of the programme and to be learnt in bite-sized chunks. Verse one is easy to pick up, with actions that match the words. It doesn't ask children who are new to church to sing words they may not believe or understand. On Day 2, verse 2 (the slow bit) reinforces the problem of sin, but reiterates that God

has a plan. At the end of Day 3 and on Day 4, learn verse 3. This is the key to God's plan as Jesus steps in. The final verse just rounds off a repeat of verse 1 with a slightly different form looking back on the week rather than forward. It ends with a joyful, shouted 'Jesus!' If nothing else sticks, pray that this will.

You may just like to use verse 1 and the final shout as the theme song for your holiday club if you merely want a very simple song which is the same every day.

MegaQuest Theme Song

The words for the song are on page 17

13

Getting your venue ready

To help the children to enter the experience of each level, you could create a different atmosphere and environment each day. It may sound a tall order to re-decorate your hall every day but don't feel daunted! There are things you can do. Check these possibilities to see if one of them matches the limitations or possibilities presented by your building and by the time and talents available to you. Don't forget there may be people who can't make the club time but who are willing to give time before or after their other commitments. For further details look on the website.

Post it — The basic techniques for each of the following suggestions are the same. They have not all been repeated for each suggestion.

Option 1 – Having one room for the Upload Zone and changing it each day.

Upload Zone

Set aside one room/space as the Upload Zone. Provided it is large enough for the number of children and team you expect (but manageably small) you can create a different look for each day using old sheets, curtains, paper and card. A camouflage net is useful (about £25 from government surplus shops), or a parachute (also available from surplus shops or, in England and Wales, subject to availability, from SU Missions). Slide and/or overhead projectors can be used to give a different scene each day.

The entrance to the room can be made to look like a computer screen. Then children can be called 'on-line' with a sound effect and a voice through a sound system which raises curiosity about each day's level.

Option 2 – Changing just the entrance into the Upload Zone – the transit corridor.

Transit corridor

Use the same sort of techniques as above to create a space through which the children are taken when it is time to move from the welcome activity and go 'on-line'. This could be a corridor, or a room which would be too small for all the children at once. Groups could go through one at a time. As they emerge they can be encouraged to describe the level and what they think it is.

Option 3 – Creating a changeable space within a larger room

Use the ideas below to create a small area within a larger room which looks different each day. This might mean just a different projected background, or it could involve the kind of evolving scenery suggested on the Scripture Union **MegaQuest** website.

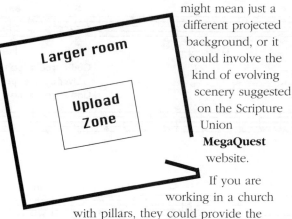

Larger room

Upload Zone

If you are working in a church with pillars, they could provide the corners of the structure. Fix ropes between them and suspend screens from which camouflage nets, old sheets or tarpaulins can be hung.

Alternatively you could borrow a scaffold tower. One domestic type scaffold tower will make two 10ft high towers, which could be two corners in a structure like the one on the website. They must be fixed firmly to a wall or similar for safety, unless you can provide stabilising struts.

The atmosphere is more controllable if a roof can be contrived (perhaps a parachute, or lengths of strong paper, sometimes available from printers on large ends-of-roll), but this is the hardest part to do.

Option 4 – Changing your stage area at the front

Front or stage area

Upload Zone

Each day change the scenery at the front (on the stage if you have one) to create a different atmosphere. The options above give some ideas.

Remember the **MegaQuest** website includes pages for people to share ideas and resources. See if someone near you has what you need and is willing to lend it.

Approaching the different levels

If you have or can borrow some lights, changing the colour of the gels from day to day can greatly alter the mood.

Level 1: **The garden**

Theme: God is the creator who created a brilliant world. We are made in God's image. God doesn't make mistakes but we do...

Colours: greens and primary colours.

Equipment: tree and plant outlines; inflatable animals and fruit to create a lush garden feel; a cosmic backcloth of stars, planets, earth, total darkness and sudden light; green camouflage nets with bright crêpe paper flowers; birdsong sound effects.

Entrance: a projected garden scene. Lights flash and a sound effect announces the start of the programme. As everyone goes into the Upload Zone, there could be darkness followed by lights suddenly coming up.

Level 2: **The mountain**

Theme: God's plan to remedy the badness in his spoilt world and the giving of the ten commandments on Sinai. Even then however, mistakes are made and God is disobeyed.

Colours: grey mystery.

Equipment: papier mâché rocks or paper sacks stuffed with newspaper and painted grey; grey drapes. Smoke, fire, dense cloud effects (smoke machines can be hired from disco or theatre suppliers or may be available from a local school), flashing lightning and thunder sound effects could also be used.

Entrance: a projected mountain scene. As the children enter the Upload Zone, lightning flashes through the mist. They can be 'roped' together being careful not to trip over the rocks as they climb the mountain.

Level 3: **The hill**

Theme: a perfect rescuer, Jesus, puts right the relationship between God and his world through his self-sacrifice. His work is complete and is for all people through all time.

Colours: brown and black.

Equipment: one or three crosses placed prominently; rocks (from level two) form a barren landscape; distant city walls; a projected view down on Jerusalem; haunting music.

Entrance: children creep in to sit around the cross(es). Blue light can give a cold feel to the scene.

Level 4: **The road**

Theme: resurrection – Jesus is alive again and we can know him personally for ourselves.

Colours: glowing reds and purples. Sunset/sunrise fills one wall.

Equipment: a road going into the distance, made by brown material verges, maybe with a roadsign; gentle music. Project a picture of Golgotha with three empty crosses onto the wall. Position the crosses from Level 3 so that they are still in view but not so prominent.

Entrance: children enter dragging their feet as if they are tired and have walked a long way.

Level 5: **The city**

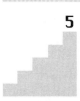

Theme: heaven, a new creation, perfection again and no more tears or suffering. I want to be there!

Colours: bright and sparkling, jewels, gold, light.

Equipment: pleasant smells; gentle or grand music playing in the background; use gold, reflective material (CDs and CD Rom freebies are ideal!). A tree of life (borrowed from level one) and something to suggest the river of life (blue crêpe paper?). Avoid being tacky and reinforcing the twee caricature of clouds, harps and halos! Try ultra-violet light (a 4ft tube will cost about £15.) However, test beforehand that the stuff you hope will reflect it, does! It's impossible to tell without trying it out.

An easier alternative to the above would be to pick up on the River and Tree theme from Revelation 22, and go back to the feel of Day 1 for 'Eden restored'.

Entrance: Children can skip in!

Practical stuff

Using an overhead projector

If you wish to use additional material from the website, or want to adapt the activity sheets, here are some ideas, along with a few suggestions for making the most of your artwork.

- If you can't find someone in your church who has internet access to download material on the website (ask around before you assume you don't), there will be computer shops and print bureaux in most towns who will do it for a fee and give you the files on a disk. For a fee, the latter will also be able to print colour visuals onto acetates for OHP or make them into slides for a slide projector. They will also be able to scan the artwork on the activity sheets so that they can be re-arranged using desk-top publishing.

- Artwork can always be re-arranged by photocopying (using the enlarge/reduce facility to resize) and using scissors and paste to make a new original. Copy shops will also undertake this kind of work for a fee.

- You can print from a computer straight onto acetates if you have the right acetates. (Note – the wrong acetates will make a terrible and expensive mess of a printer or photocopier so check before you do this.) Song slides made like this are much preferable to handwritten. Include suitable artwork, but don't make the words hard to read. When making acetates remember that nearly all screens are either square or landscape format, so make your acetates to match.

- Inkjet acetates remain vulnerable to moisture, and fingerprints are impossible to remove. Any activity with children generates both! Totally clear plastic wallets are available which protect acetates during use. Do not put them in until the ink is fully dry or both will be unusable.

- Use card to frame your projection for a better effect. The easiest way is to tape four strips of card to the OHP, and just lay your acetates on top. For one frame to work for all, all the acetates must be the same size and orientation. Alternatively, frame each acetate (you can buy frames), especially if you will use them a lot. They are much easier to handle, and the frame can be used to write notes that only you can see.

Using a computer

It may help the computer 'feel' of the club to make use of some of the following ideas. None is essential! These are simply suggestions.

- Co-ordinate all your projections of song words and visuals using a computer linked to a LCD panel on your OHP.

- Use a computer to register children. At one of the pilot clubs a computer-studies student wrote a programme to convert the names to bar-codes. We put the codes on a badge with their names and they were scanned as they arrived on subsequent days. The children loved it and someone who otherwise may not have felt he had anything to offer to the club was able to contribute. It was a very reliable way of keeping a register without anyone checking through a list, or needing to transfer or collate names.

- Have an email post-box for jokes and questions, with computers available for children to use. This does not require real internet connection or network to simulate.

- Email well-known Christians with a question about God's BIG plan, or ask how they became Christians. Email the central office of your denomination and see if you can get permission for children to email a well-known Christian leader – and expect some sort of reply. Or you can set up a list of the addresses of people in your own church or well-known Christians in your locality who are prepared to be contacted by email.

- Depending on numbers you may be able to have one group per day using good quality Christian software instead of a craft time. Check the suitability and quality of the software.

Using video

The video which has been produced for **MegaQuest** contains excellent resource material. Of course using a video does have some drawbacks alongside the advantages. But they are not usually insurmountable.

- *It's not too difficult.* Setting up a VCR and TV, plus a couple of extra TVs for larger groups is not technically difficult. You should have someone in your church who can do it for you. If the group is large enough you will need a sound system. Route the audio signal from the VCR through it. Even if you have a smaller group, try to use amplification. The sound quality produced by TV sets is the biggest problem when showing a video in a larger room, especially if the acoustics of your hall are poor.

- *It's not too expensive.* The video is a reusable resource which can be a part of your regular teaching programme. **MegaQuest**, God's BIG plan for the world is not so tightly tied in with the holiday club material that it cannot be used on its own. It contains a powerful retelling of five of the biggest stories in the Bible. TVs can be borrowed, or hired cheaply from a second-hand electrical shop, or bought cheaply from an auction. You could build a video-wall from second-hand TV's if you wanted. Three large sets are adequate for around 100, so long as you've amplified the sound

separately. (Video projectors are expensive, and need good blackout, but some churches and schools have them. They can sometimes be borrowed. Handle carefully however. The bulbs in most cost around £300.)

- *It's not too impersonal.* Just sitting children in front of a screen can be impersonal. Using the professional skills of writer, artist and actor can be very valuable as part of a programme, when team leaders sit with children to share the video experience. Most children see so much video that they can get easily bored. But they do not see much television that is shared with an interested adult.

Post it

Do check in advance that:
- you have adequate light-restricting facilities to avoid reflection from the screens
- every child can see
- the video is working and set at the right starting point each day.

Song words

Clap your hands and wave them about

Stamp your feet on the floor and get ready to shout *(Leader [spoken] 'Alright?' All shout, 'Alright!')*

God's got a plan for his world that we're here to find out

It's no great mystery now the secret is out

God made the world and he saw it was good

but people like us didn't do what we should

the world was spoiled by all that's gone wrong

but God had a plan that's why we're singing this song

Jesus came to put it all right

He's God's Son and he overcame darkness with light *(Leader [spoken] 'Alright?' All shout, 'Alright!')*

Lived the perfect life the way it should be

He died for us, then rose so we can be free

Clap your hands and wave them about

Stamp your feet on the floor and get ready to shout *(Leader [spoken] 'Alright?' All shout, 'Alright!')*

God's got a plan for his world that's what we've found out

So let everybody know the secret is out

So let's shout JESUS!

Artwork

Artwork for Day 1

Artwork for Day 3

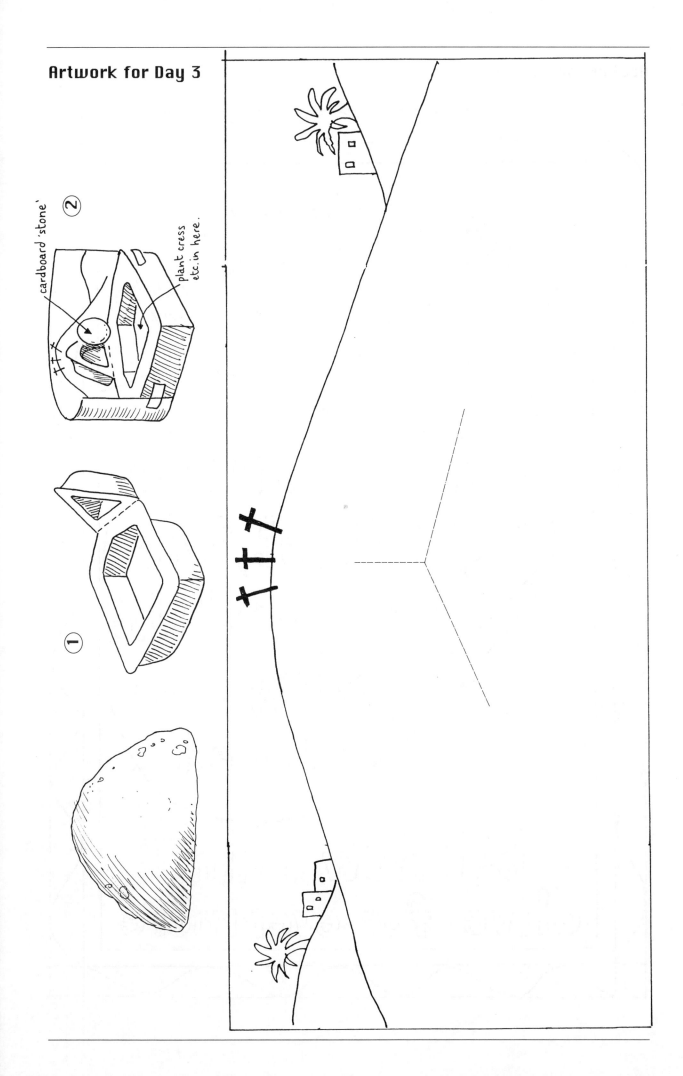

② cardboard 'stone'

plant cress etc. in here.

①

Artwork for Day 5

MegaQuest logo

Pogo Challenge

This game attempts to replicate one of those computer games where the hero leaps and grabs things in the sky, scoring points or getting zapped. The main idea is to suspend balloons, half of which contain points to collect (Smarties work well), while the rest are booby-trapped with such things as water, talc, flour, gunge or whatever is suitable. Contestants jump up to try to pop the balloons using a hat with a small pin attached.

Suspend the balloons from a length of plastic guttering. Drill 1/2 cm holes about 20cm apart along the length of the guttering. Blown up and filled balloons are suspended by pushing the knotted end through from the concave side.

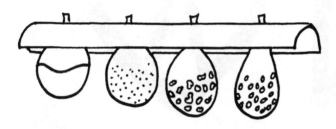

When the whole structure is 'loaded', find a suitable adjustable mechanism for suspending it so that it suits the height of the contestants – a gantry with pulleys or a person at each end. The curve of the guttering holds the balloons firmly enough for the pin to pop them and can be removed for loading and kept out of harm's way until needed.

For the hats, either use baseball caps, with a drawing pin stitched to the top, an old plastic helmet, a toy helmet or an old cycle helmet. The pin can be attached with tape. If it has no peak make one from card so that contestants can't easily see which balloons are booby-trapped. It also keeps powder and gunge out of eyes. The hats need to adjust to a range of head sizes and stay on firmly!

Contestants can either simply jump or use some kind of bouncer such as a space-hopper or pogo-sticks (for older children) or even a small trampoline if you have one. Children can volunteer or names can be picked from a 'hat'. Use the Pogo Challenge as often as is appropriate during **MegaQuest**.

Drama

The Virus Buster

From an original idea and scripts by Jane Mitchell. Particular thanks to the three troupes who tried it out and for their thoughts. Special thanks to Nigel Styles for suggestions for episodes 1 and 5.

Cast

Logoff: a cartoon baddy. There should be plenty of slapstick between him and Dum Dum. When he appears, the audience should be encouraged to boo or hiss although make sure they quieten down so his lines can be heard.

DumDum: Logoff's dumb sidekick

Programmer/Alathos

Super-Harryo: Harryo is not bright and could have a stagey Italian accent .

Cronic: is in a hurry to get on.

Flora Cruft: is gung-ho.

Super Harryo, Cronic and Flora are stereotypical games characters and are esentially 'goodies'.

Notes

- If finding six actors is a problem, the three 'goodies' can be reduced to two by removing Cronic. Redistribute the lines and ensure that references to him are removed!

- Competent drama groups may prefer to improvise from a plot summary rather than a script. One is available on the **MegaQuest** website. The drama script appears in full on the website so that if your group needs to amend the script, it can be downloaded and edited as appropriate.

- If your club is less than five days, you may wish to use the appropriate episode at a family evening or something similar during the week, or at a Sunday service. If you have a five day club and want to present the final episode at a Sunday service, you could do episode 4 in two parts on consecutive days. It is split into Part A and Part B.

- If your drama team is coming in specially to do the sketch each day, you may prefer to run 4A and 4B together.

Episode 1

Props: *balloons; bottle labelled 'virus'*

Opening scene: *Programmer sitting at computer, possibly with back to audience (a microphone can ensure everyone will hear him) or silhouetted against a light, so that the identity of Alathos as the Programmer is not immediately obvious until episode 3. The poses adopted by Flora, Cronic and Harryo during this introduction should be grossly exaggerated and repeated frequently as appropriate during the rest of the story when they speak. Balloons, some filled with water or with other substances, are lying around like fruit for the three heroes to encounter. A 'No entry' sign is pinned to the door of a 'cave'.*

Programmer: At last! The ultimate programming task is completed. I, the Programmer, have written the perfect code for a game which includes the best of all possible games. The ultimate heroes – brave, but human – Flora Cruft *(enter Flora who poses and freezes)* fast, but brainy; a cross between Croc and Sonic ... Cronic *(enter Cronic ditto)* and *(enter Harryo looking dumb and then freezing in position)* how shall I put it? A suitable contrast to those two: Super Harryo 6.4. We need some humour after all! And they're not controlled by some joystick-happy control-freak.

They're free. Free to explore and enjoy all the levels imaginable in the programme. And now, for the moment I've worked so hard for – to set the programme running and to see it work... *(He presses a button.)* It's very good! Time for a cup of tea, I think. *(Exit.)*

The three characters unfreeze and look around.

Flora: Wow. Look what's happened! One minute a jumble of bits and bytes and then suddenly it's beautiful! Let's start gathering fruits. Maybe there'll be a bonus.

23

Harryo: A bone for us? Why? We aren't dogs...

Flora: No, not...

Cronic: We've no time to waste explaining stuff to him. Let's get on and explore. We could go this way, or that way, or that way, or that way. Or what about that door, or up that cliff, or I could jump through that cave or...

Harryo: What's it say on that cave? I don't read too well.

Flora: It says 'No entry' with the Programmer's logo on it. I don't think we should go that way.

Cronic: OK, let's go this way and gather strength from these fruit. *(He leads off, popping/gathering balloons and shouting with delight. He's followed by Harryo who pops one that is filled with water/flour. Flora exits last, laughing.)*

Enter Logoff and DumDum carrying a big bottle subtly labelled 'virus'. Boos, hisses etc. DumDum should actively participate in the next speech, repeating bits and generally hamming it up.

Logoff: So here we are, inside the programme. *(He turns to the audience.)* And you lot can shut up! I am Logoff, and soon you'll see why! Our virus will log everything off! Our evil master slipped us into the code while the Programmer was making tea. And now all we have to do is introduce the virus into the programme and it will all be ruined. Ha! Ha! Ha! Check the virus, DumDum. *(DumDum makes to drink out of the bottle.)* Stop, you fool! Check it like this!

'Virus, virus, do your thing, Come out of the bottle and work your ruin.' I made that up all by myself! *(DumDum repeats, gets it wrong and gets hit. When he's got it right, he tries to pour out the virus.)* Stop! We can't ruin it ourselves. We aren't part of the Programmer's code. We've got to get one of those goody-goodies he's invented to do that. And we shall have to be clever to get them to 'co-operate'. Or rather I shall have to be clever (the easy part) and you'll have to do what you're told. Let's see if we can find them. I wonder what level they're on... *(He sees the audience.)* O look there are people out there! I love an audience! Hello worms. You're very privileged you know – you are about to witness my victory and the triumph of my evil master. Eventually we shall take over the whole world through computers, so you'd better be prepared to do what I say. I'll have access to the computers they use to write your school reports soon! Heh heh. *(Boos etc.)* Come on DumDum.

DumDum: Yes Your Evil Highness. *(after he's gone)* No Your Evil Highness. Three bags full Your Evil Highness. Still it'll be fun when the virus gets into the system and ruins everything. I like spoiling things. I like scribbling on bits of nice, white paper. I like dribbling down clean clothes. And I really, really like...

Logoff: *(re-entering)* You're dumber than that brainless Harryo. But your heart's in the wrong place so you'll do. *(DumDum searches around for his heart. Logoff hits him.)* Stop

being stupid! Now come on! *(They start to leave.)* Come to think of it you've given me an idea! I think we shall try to work on Harryo the brainbox. He's at least one microchip short of the full butty. We should be able to get him to introduce the virus no problem...

Voice-over *(a la 1960's Batman show):* Will Cronic ever stop to think? Will Harryo ever start to think? Will the virus ruin everything, or has the acting already done that? *(etc.)*

Episode 2

Props: *virus bottle*

Logoff: *(Enters with DumDum: Boos, hisses etc.)* Good morning worms! I see you have returned to see my wonderful plot come to fruition. It's nice to see such dedication in such an ugly bunch. You must be more intelligent than you look. Soon I shall have corrupted the system with my Automatic Transmogrifying ASCII... Oh, all right, let's call it a virus. It might not be such a grand title, but at least your teeth don't fall out while you're trying to say it. Now DumDum – here's the plan. They'll trust you, so I'll keep out of the way. We want them to let the virus loose and the best place for it is just there. *(Points to 'No entry' sign.)* That logo gives me the creeps...

DumDum: What, the Programmer's...

Logoff: Don't mention that name to me. When we find them you must persuade them that nothing bad will happen if they break the Programmer's rules. Better still, they must think it will be good for them. Little will they see how the virus will spread and spread and corrupt the whole programme. There'll be chaos! There'll be disaster! It'll be worse than a rainy day in *(name your place)*!!

DumDum: Er... Your... Mouldiness.

Logoff: Shut up! Don't interrupt your elders and worsers. Especially when I'm getting carried away...

DumDum: *(aside)* I wish he would get carried away

Logoff: What did you say?

DumDum: I said er er, 'Hip hip hooray.' But I think someone's coming.

Logoff: Ah it looks like our poor little friends are on their way. Stop wasting time with your stupid boasting and speechifying, DumDum. Let's hide and see what they do. *(They run off.)*

Cronic, Harryo and Flora enter.

Cronic: Wow this is brilliant. I've scored 60 squillion points already and we haven't found anyone to zap. Let's go!

Flora: No! Let's stop and think for a bit. My body's tired out.

Harryo: No!!! Let's stop and NOT think for a while. My body and my brain are tired out.

Flora: I wonder why we're not allowed to go that way. I'd love to try it and see. But if...

Harryo: Maybe it would just be bad for us.

Cronic: Maybe, maybe, maybe. Let's get on and do something. *(DumDum has sidled up behind Cronic and, as Cronic turns, they collide.)*

Flora: Who are you? Hands up or I'll let you have it. Oh I'd forgotten. The Programmer didn't give me anything to let anyone have anything with. I'm supposed to get on with other people... But who are you anyway?

DumDum: A friend ... not like that Programmer you just mentioned. He just wants to spoil your fun. Why d'you think he told you not to go into the best part of the game?

Cronic: Is it really the best part? Down through that cave?

Flora: Is it really exciting.

DumDum: *(hesitating)* I don't really know...

Logoff: *(from off-stage, in stage whisper)* No you idiot. Don't hesitate. Whatever the question, the answer's yes. Don't worry about the truth.

DumDum: I don't really know ... how to tell you just how exciting it is. *(Repeating after Logoff, as above.)* You'll be just like the Programmer yourselves if you achieve that level. And especially if you pour this pot of vi..er Automatic Transmogrifying ASCII-disrupting Neutron er, er, stuff into the er, hardware/software interface bus module er, er, thingy, to er, speed it all up.

Harryo: He's very brainy isn't he? I didn't understand a word of that so it must be clever. But I still don't think we should do what the Programmer says we shouldn't!

Flora: But think of the thrills!

Cronic: And think of the speed with that auto train nuclear bus module er.. what was the last technical bit?

DumDum: Thingy.

Harryo: Thingy! He's brilliant. But I still say we shouldn't do it.

Cronic: With the thingy to speed it all up. Just try and stop me. *(He grabs the virus and runs off, past the sign.)*

Flora: We'll be all right. It's just a little sign. I can hardly see it. *(She runs off, covering the sign with her hand.)*

Harryo: But... I hope it'll be all right. *(He walks slowly off in the other direction.)* Somehow I think we should have done things the Programmer's way...

Logoff: *(enters)* Brilliant! Brilliant!! Brilliant!!!

DumDum: Thanks it was noth...

Logoff: Not you, you miserable worm. Me. What a great plan. It's all doomed! The Programmer has been foiled! It's only a matter of time before it all falls to pieces. *(Boos etc.)* And you lot can shut up, you miserable worms. I hate children. In fact I hate anything and everything. Come here DumDum. I need something to kick while I'm waiting for the virus to start working. They can't stop it now. We've won.

Harryo: *(re-entering)* Oh no! I'm starting to feel strange. The virus is already working. I wish I knew how to contact the

Programmer. He's the only one who may be able to save the whole system. O mamma mia! My hat is starting to warp, my legs don't follow each other properly *(staggers around)*. It won't be long before my programme crashes.

Voice-over: Will we ever see Flora and Cronic again? Will Harryo's legs ever follow one another? Come to think of it: *did* they follow one another in the first place? Has Logoff out-virussed the Programmer? Will *(actor's name)* ever remember his/her lines? *(etc.)*

Episode 3

Props: *sheet for maze (optional)*

Enter Harryo, Flora and Cronic. The set looks decrepit.

Flora: I feel terrible. And everything is falling apart. If only we hadn't disobeyed the Programmer and let the virus loose in the system. If I see that creep who gave us the virus, I'll blast him out of the programme.

Harryo: I think we'd be better off finding the Programmer.

Cronic: You *think!* That's a good one.

Flora: I don't think we should be making fun of Harryo, when we were the ones who fell for the stupid story about the Programmer. You know – that he had only stopped us going into that cave because he wanted us to have fun.

Cronic: Yeah, OK. I'm sorry. But how are we going to find the Programmer? And will he want to help us after what we've done?

Flora: Maybe we should forget about the Programmer and deal with the problem ourselves.

Cronic: Let's go! *(Flora and Cronic exit.)*

Harryo: I still think I'm not as stupid as they say. And we're wasting our time unless the Programmer helps us. But since I don't know how to find him, I'll go with the others. Perhaps they'll need me. *(He exits.)*

Logoff: *(enters with DumDum)* How many times have I got to tell you. No!

DumDum: But I haven't had a day off for five years.

Logoff: And you're not having one now. I know you just want

to go along to that **MegaQuest** holiday club. I'm not having you mixing with that lot! They'll be a bad influence on you. You might start being good. So be a bad DumDum and shut up. *(DumDum makes faces behind Logoff's back, but Logoff never quite catches him.)*

Enter Flora, Cronic and Harryo.

Cronic: Hey this is the next level. I don't like it. And who are they? The big (small/fat/blond etc.) one looks horrible. Hey that's the smooth-talking dude who talked us into putting the virus into the system.

Flora: I'll get him. *(There follows a big corny chase around the room. All exit. Logoff and DumDum re-enter.)*

Logoff: Good – they've followed us. Now we're here in

the Maze Zone. Let's see them get out of that. *(He exits. DumDum gets members of the audience to be the walls of the maze. It could be all of the children standing with arms out as in a game of Cat and Mouse. If space is tight use a few volunteers, or get a couple of adults to hold a large sheet or similar, behind which the characters disappear and get lost, sticking their heads out at different points to speak. The others enter.)*

Flora: Which way now? *(They all go off in different directions, or behind the 'sheet'.)*

Cronic: Harryo, where are you?

Harryo: I don't know. All these passages look the same.

Flora: Can you see the way out? Help! Help!

Logoff: *(enters one side with DumDum)* Ha! All we need to do now is cover them with this anti-interface dust. It'll really slow them down until the virus is fully working. Here DumDum. Get ready to take it in. *(They busy themselves with the dust. Alathos enters on the other side.)*

Alathos: Here. I'll help you out. I know the way. Follow me. *(He rescues all of them. As they stand outside the maze DumDum enters it.)*

DumDum: I can't find them.

Logoff: How can they possibly have found their way out without help? And who could help them but the Programmer? What! There they are! Leaving this level! And who is that with them?

Alathos: *(looking across at Logoff)* Logoff, you won't succeed. I am Alathos.

Logoff: Alathos?

Alathos: Yes, Alathos. I have come from the Programmer *(Logoff yells in pain at the sound of the name and covers his ears.)* You have no power over me. Go! *(Logoff moves to side, snarling and Alathos turns to Flora, Harryo and Cronic.)* Come with me. *(They leave.)*

DumDum: Help! Your Mouldiness. You didn't show me how to get out of the maze.

Logoff: *(ignoring him and mimicking Alathos)* 'You won't succeed'. O yes I will. *(Encourage the audience in pantomime style 'O no you won't' etc.)*

DumDum: Pleeeeeease!! I can't get out.

Logoff: Must I do everything for you, you twerp. *(He carries him out and puts him down.)* Now come on.

DumDum: This dust makes my nose itch... atchoo *(He sneezes dust over Logoff.)*

Logoff: Fool. You'll pay for this! *(to audience)* And you lot can stop laughing as well. Just wait till I control the computer that runs all the traffic lights in *(name your place)*. *(Both exit.)*

Flora: *(entering with Alathos, Cronic and Harryo)* Have you really been sent by the Programmer?

Alathos: Yes... the virus can only be destroyed from inside the system. Will you help me?

Cronic: But we let the virus loose.

Alathos: I know that. But I've

come to destroy it.

Flora: We're really sorry...

Alathos: If you're sorry, come with me.

Harryo: You try and stop me! I knew we needed the Programmer's help. *(Exit Alathos and Harryo.)*

Flora: Hey this is heavy. Do you think Alathos could be the Programmer himself?

Cronic: I haven't got time to decide about that. How could the Programmer be in his own programme? But I'm going with him. There's something about him. I trust him. *(They exit.)*

Voice-over: Can the virus be stopped? Can Alathos make Logoff log off? Is anyone as dumb as DumDum? Or is DumDum dumber than them all? Will we find out what makes DumDum dumb *(He breaks into a tune dumdumdum...eg theme song.)* O sorry, I forgot where I was. O yes! The really big question: who is Alathos?... *(Whole cast, from off: Alathos?!)* Yes. Who is Alathos?

Episode 4

Props: *aerobics music to play at the beginning; water pistol; Alathos' computer keyboard.*

Part A

Enter Flora and Cronic, exercising to an aerobics tape. They get some (all?) of the audience to join in. Enter Harryo.

Harryo: What on earth are you two doing?

Cronic: Keeping fit. No good getting out of shape with Logoff threatening our every megabyte, is there?

Harryo: But do you think it'll do any good?

Flora: Of course! That ugly dude had better not mess with me or I'll pull his ears out of shape and use his nose as a can-opener.

Harryo: Aren't you a bit frightened?

Flora: Flora Cruft is afraid of no one.

Cronic: Where's Alathos?

Harryo: He's off sorting out some of the things the virus has messed up. He says our interface is out of phase, our icons are 'I can'ts' and our real-time 3D animated morphing is er..er.. not working properly.

Flora: Let's go and sort some of them out ourselves.

Harryo: What! On our own? What if we get into trouble? If Alathos hadn't found us yesterday we'd never have got out of the maze. I wonder who

he really is.

Flora: Don't worry: I'm with you.

Cronic: Yeah. Let's go. I can't stand standing around. The only thing I can't stand more than standing around is sitting around. I really can't sit that at all. Come on.

Harryo: I don't like it. *(All exit.)*

Enter Logoff.

Logoff: Good morning worms. Have I told you I eat worms, by the way? Hmm... some of you look very tasty. Especially that one there. Can I see you later? Would you like to come for a meal? I'm feeling a little peckish. Ha! Ha! *(Enter DumDum.)* Oh, it's you. What do you want?

DumDum: Our anti-anti-virus software reports that Alathos is repairing what the virus is ruining, your Royal Foulity.

Logoff: Try to get all the corrupted programmes to work at once. That'll hold him up. And we must find a way of getting to him. Where are the troublesome threesome he rescued the other day?

DumDum: They seem to be alone, master. They're trying to do what Alathos is doing. But they're no good at it yet.

Logoff: Good. This is my chance to get rid of them. Fetch my disruptor gun. I'll blast them into their component parts. Come DumDum, my little rotten pomegranate, I may need some

aid to distract them. *(Exit)*

DumDum: Some aid? I had some lemonade, but I drank it. Maybe Logoff has some more. *(He exits.)*

Enter Harryo, Cronic, Flora.

Harryo: It's no good. We can't sort out the introfuses or the pie cans or the 3B mighty-morphing whatsit thingies without help from Alathos.

Flora: Perhaps you're right. There's more to him than meets the eye. He's no ordinary programme, even for one sent by the Programmer

Cronic: You think too much. Thinking is bad for the digestion and it stunts rapid motor reactions in the muscles. At least that's what I think.

Harryo: I thought you didn't think.

Cronic: No I think I think thinking about things too much thins things I think should be thicker.

Harryo: I wish I hadn't asked. Let's go back.

Enter Logoff and DumDum.

Logoff: Not so fast my friends, you shouldn't have come so far on your own.

Flora runs at him, is tripped by DumDum. Cronic runs off, is shot with a water pistol and falls.

Harryo: What have you done to him?

Logoff: Scattered his programme all over the system.

You two are going to come with me. You have information I require about Alathos.

Flora: Why do you want to know about him?

Logoff: Even he *(points to Harryo)* can't have failed to notice that he is no ordinary programmer. Bring them DumDum. To my headquarters.

All exit, except Cronic who lies colllapsed on the floor. Enter Alathos. He goes to Cronic, looks at him and gets out a keyboard or calculator. After a few seconds, Cronic gets up.

Cronic: I feel most strange. What happened?

Alathos: Your programme was terminated. Logoff tried to trash you.

Cronic: Then how...

Alathos: I retrieved you.

Cronic: I've got to ask you. Who are you really?

Alathos: Who do you think?

Cronic: If you can do that, there's only one answer. You must be the Programmer.

Alathos: Well done Cron, you're right.

Cronic: But why are you in here?

Alathos: It was the only way.

Cronic: But...

Alathos: Enough questions. We must go and rescue the others. *(Exit.)*

Cronic: Well that's news. I wonder what happens now. *(Exit.)*

Part B

Enter DumDum.

DumDum: Hello worms. Ha! Ha! *(imitates Logoff)* Hello worms!

Logoff: *(enters)* What did you say?

DumDum: I said 'Hello worms'. It's what you always say to that lot out there.

Logoff: Precisely. It's what *I* always say. You're getting a bit above yourself. I shall have to teach you a lesson. I'll send you to *(name a suitable place)* for a holiday!

DumDum: O no, please!! I'll be good!

Logoff: But I don't want you to be good DumDum. I want you to be evil. It's no good hissing and booing at me! I love boos. It shows I'm doing a good job. I know you all wanted the goody-goodies to win. But I've put an end to one of them already. I disrupted him good and proper with a fatal error didn't I? He's crashed, he is no more. *(If the children don't heckle, one of the team needs to start them...)* What! He's still active. Who brought him back? Nobody can do that.

DumDum: Except the Programmer.

Logoff: Aaah! Don't say that. Alathos can't be the Programmer. Not here in the system. Or can he? Fetch the prisoners.

DumDum brings on Harryo and Flora. Flora rushes forward.

Flora: I'll sort you out.

Logoff: Do shut up, or I'll trash you immediately. You have information I require about the one who calls himself Alathos.

Flora and Harryo: Alathos?

Logoff: Yes Alathos, although I begin to suspect he has other names.

Flora: Like what, you monster?

Logoff: Like the Programmer, maybe. *(His voice and face show pain at the P word.)*

Harryo: The Programmer! I wish I'd known. I could have asked him to...

Logoff: It's too late for that. It's too late for anything. You have jumped your last level, and you, my dear, have fought your last battle.

Flora: You can't delete me. I'm a heroine. You can't. Please don't. Please!

Logoff: Now she starts to fear. Like all programmes when you face the final level your courage disappears. Come with me. I must plan.

All exit. Enter Cronic and Alathos.

Cronic: What are we going to do.

Alathos: The others are in great danger.

Cronic: But you can save them, like you saved me.

Alathos: It may not be so easy. Logoff has them in his headquarters where the disruption is greatest. *(to audience)* What does Logoff plan? ... It is decided. I will go and fetch them. Wait here. I will return.

Cronic: I'm going to follow. I hope he won't be angry. *(Exit. Enter Logoff and prisoners.)*

Logoff: I can't stand all this waiting. Where in the system is DumDum?

DumDum: *(entering)* Logoff sir... Alathos is coming this way... He looks really determined. Save me, save me! *(He hides behind Logoff.)*

Logoff: Stop cringing, you ridiculous robot. Get out from behind me. Get in front of me. No, better still, we'll both get behind this lot. *(Enter Alathos.)*

Alathos: I wish to speak with you, Logoff.

Logoff: What do you want?

Alathos: I have come for Harryo and Flora. Release them.

Logoff: Why should I do that?

Alathos: I will give you something in return.

Logoff: What could you possibly give me in return?

Alathos: Myself. I will take their place.

Harryo: Don't do it Alathos. We're not worth it.

Alathos: I'll decide that. I made you.

Logoff: So you are the Programmer.

Alathos: Yes. Now release

them. Go all of you.

Flora: But what about you.

Alathos: Go! *(Exit Flora and Harryo.)*

Logoff: Victory! At last. I cannot believe you are such a fool. To sacrifice yourself for those worms. And now you are in my power. In the system I have corrupted, you have all the weaknesses of a mere programme. And with you out of the way who will challenge my rule? No one. You have given me control of the system for ever.

Exit all.

Voice-over: *ad lib.*

Episode 5

Props: *keyboard; water pistol; tray of plates and cups.*

Enter Logoff and DumDum. Plenty of slapstick as they celebrate.

Logoff: Victory! Oh it's so wonderful. I am the ruler of the system and everyone is going to do what I say... O hello worms. You see I told you I'd win. You didn't believe me but you were wrong. So, Ha! Ha! Ha! Now to start with I'll have all your bikes, your Nintendos and your Playstations...oh and your car keys you lot at the back! I love a good gloat. Jolly good gloating weather. *(He exits.)*

Enter Harryo, Flora and Cronic.

Flora: Stop! It's no use. I can't run any further.

Harryo: But we must. Logoff will be after us as soon as he's finished with Alathos.

Cronic: Poor Alathos. I don't think we'll be seeing him again, in spite of what he said.

Flora: Why, what did he say?

Cronic: He said he'd be back. Just before he came to rescue you. He seemed very certain of it.

Harryo: He expected to be deleted. You could see it in his eyes.

Cronic: We can always hope.

Flora: There is no hope, Cron. It's no good kidding yourself.

Harryo: Come on we must keep moving.

Flora: What's the point? Logoff will get us eventually.

Harryo: We mustn't give up, Flora.

Cronic: Maybe there's another game.

Flora: But now we've met the Programmer, nothing else will do. I'm just going to sit and wait.

Cronic: What for?

Flora: I really don't know. *(They all sit down. Enter Logoff and DumDum.)*

Logoff: Well that's that dealt with. The Programmer is no more. We'd better speak to all the programmes. Give them a fair choice. Serve me or be deleted. That's the sort of thing.

DumDum: *(handing him the Programmer's keyboard)* And what shall we do with this?

Logoff: Ah now I really have the Programmer's power... let's see. What's this... it's registering the virus activity... the virus is dying. DumDum, what have you done? *(He hits him lots.)* You've deleted the virus as well as Alathos!

DumDum: Please master. I didn't... *(Enter Alathos.)*

Programmer: Don't blame him Logoff. It was my doing.

Logoff: But... but... but it can't be. You're crashed, deleted, trashed, wiped, removed from RAM.

Alathos: It was all planned. I programmed myself to return knowing you would delete me, and I took the virus with me. Now any programme who wishes it, can have the virus wiped right off their disk. Your power is broken and the programmes can go on to even higher levels. Each one better than the last in a game that goes on for ever! *(He exits)*

Logoff: But you can't do that.

DumDum: You look logged-off Logoff.

Logoff: I'm really logged off. And I'll log you off for good too. After him DumDum. *(Logoff exits.)*

Harryo: You don't have to go with him.

DumDum: What do you mean?

Flora: You could join us.

DumDum: What after all I've done?

Cronic: We've all had to be forgiven for different things. I'm sure you can be too.

Logoff: *(from off)* Come on DumDum!

Harryo: Don't go!

DumDum: I won't! *(All rejoice. Re-enter Alathos.)*

Cronic: Alathos!

Alathos: I'm sorry to keep you waiting.

Flora: But what happened?

Programmer: Logoff deleted me, but I programmed myself to return. Now the root of the virus is dead. You don't need to be afraid of it or Logoff anymore.

Harryo: Well let's celebrate!

Cronic: Yeah I'm starving.

Alathos: *(producing a tray of plates and cups)* Here we are. Eat and drink!

Enter Logoff.

Logoff: How dare you have an unauthorised party in my system! And what are you doing DumDum?

DumDum: Er, er...

Alathos: Remember you don't have to be afraid.

Logoff: Take that. *(He fires water pistol. At first they fall back.)*

DumDum: It's the virus!

Harryo: No it's not. It's just water!

DumDum: I'm not frightened of him anymore!

Harryo: Are you following this? I'm not. I don't understand any of it, but I'm glad it's happening.

Flora: Yeah let's get him! *(Custard pies and water are delivered.)*

Alathos: *(to Logoff)* Now go! *(Exit Logoff.)*

Harryo: Aren't you going to destroy him completely?

Alathos: That will come. He has lost the battle. The virus is dead, but all the programmes will face a choice. If you go my way I will always be with you and the game will go on.

All: To levels new and better.

Alathos: Better than you could ever dream. *(Exit all. Tumultuous applause etc.)*

Entry Level:
The garden

Aim

To discover that God created a perfect world which included all people, made in his own image. God planned it this way. He doesn't make mistakes.

Post it

It is important that these truths underlie all you do and teach on the first day. You may be able to study these verses together as a team. If not, ensure that this is part of each individual team member's preparation.

Bible Base: Genesis 1,2, Hebrews 1:3; 1 Peter 1:20

The substance of the teaching material is from Genesis. But we need to understand from the New Testament references that God's plan of salvation was in place before the fall – before even the creation. The cross is therefore implicit in the act of creation. The God of creation is one who created in order to redeem. God's goodness is shown in two ways:

- he made the world which includes human beings who bear his image.
- he rescues his fallen world which includes the restoration of those who bear his image but have allowed sin to spoil it.

Nothing takes God by surprise nor can anything take his world (or us) out of the scope of his BIG Plan.

You will need

- Video episode 1 or visuals for Soundbyte 1. The visuals can be found on the **MegaQuest** website.

- Cards for the Interactivity Creation Swap

- Materials for the crafts – the holographs

- Activity sheet 1 and pencils/felt-tips

- Screen picture 1 of something in creation. You can use the picture from the activity sheet for Day 1. It will need to be enlarged.

Welcome

Children arrive, are registered (see page 10), and are welcomed into their groups with lively music (have the band or a tape/CD) playing. Name badges should also be made or distributed at this point. Group leaders introduce the idea of constructing a model computer and make a start (see page 6). This is a key time for working on relationships between group members and leaders. Up-front leaders should make a point of going round the groups to chat, encourage and introduce themselves. A time-keeper must keep an eye on registration, and give group leaders notice when it is time to go 'on-line' into the Upload Zone.

Post it

"We're glad to see so many of you here. Don't worry, you've got all week to finish those computers. It's time now to go on-line into the Upload Zone, to find the first entry level of MegaQuest: God's BIG Plan for the World!"

On-line in the Upload Zone

If you establish the practice of groups sitting together from the start, it will save shuffling around if there is an Interactivity or group game during the on-line time. It is also far better for leaders to sit among the children rather than around the edge. A tap on the shoulder is far more effective at inhibiting anti-social behaviour and less distracting for others, than intervention from afar!

Sing

Teach the first verse of the theme song: emphasising that **MegaQuest** is about God's BIG Plan.

Pogo challenge

See page 22

Video/Soundbyte

Use the first episode of the **MegaQuest** video or use Soundbyte outline 1 on page 35.

The Interactivity:

Creation Swaps

Prepare pairs of creation cards. These could each contain half of something God made, or (for older children) the pairs could be of matching things created on the same day. For example, sun/moon, fish/birds. Either give each group a complete set, and race to match the pairs correctly, or if you have room for some running around, give each group a pile of the

same cards. On the word go each group tries to swap one card with each other group to get a complete set, and then match them up. You might need to adjust the numbers of groups and piles of cards; perhaps by dividing large groups or giving spare piles to extra adults who join in the game.

The sets of cards can later be displayed in group bases as a reminder.

Group time

Aim:

- To chat further informally about what a great God he must be to make such a brilliant world, how he made each of us special and unique and made us to be like him.

- To build relationships.

Activity sheet:

The activity sheet contains a number of items to follow up the video or talk. While the children use it, continue to talk with individuals. It is useful to have a system whereby the group leader can decide precisely when the group time ends, perhaps by sending a runner to fetch the drinks, or taking the group out to the refreshment area.

Refreshment break

Games

As appropriate and if time allows.

Craft

Holograph pictures

You will need:

- Artwork (see page 18). Use a computer or photocopier to make the images an appropriate size for each age-group (credit-card size for older groups, larger for younger). You could frame the images in a circle, square or rectangle.

- Foil (Cooking foil works, but specialist foil is available from art shops if your budget permits. Cut to slightly larger than the artwork.)

- Card (For mounting. Cut to size of foil.)

- Tape, glue and/or paper clips for fixing during activity and final mounting.

Felt-tips are no good for this activity.

- Pencils (fairly sharp) or ball-pens.

- Newspaper (enough for each child to be able to rest on a thickish wad).

Method

Place foil (shiny side down) on newspaper. Place artwork face up on top of the foil and fix in place with tape or clips. Trace firmly over the artwork to transfer image onto foil as raised lines which will catch the light. Varied firmness while shading can produce attractive 3D effects. When complete, turn over the foil and mount on card.

Mounting the foil on card is vital or the finished work will soon resemble a screwed up chocolate biscuit foil wrapper!

Back in the Upload Zone

This second time together will include the first episode of *The Virus Buster*, a repeat of the song, maybe another Pogo Challenge and, if it seems appropriate, a prayer of thanks for the amazing world God created.

Take the opportunity to explain briefly what you're doing when you pray, and that Amen means 'I agree', so we shouldn't say it if we don't agree, or if we haven't been listening because we won't know what we're agreeing to!

Soundbyte 1

Genesis 1,2

Visuals to use for the talk outlines can be downloaded from the **MegaQuest** website to make your own acetates.

If your club consists mainly of churched children you may feel you don't need to major on creation. If so, finish the talk by briefly telling the story of how Adam and Eve disobeyed God. However, for an outreach club, God as creator is an important bedrock to establish. The concept of sin can be introduced on Day 2.

You will need:

- One picture for each 'day' in the process of creation, with a pair, eg fish/bird on each – see the Interactivities.

- An acetate of a photograph of yourself, preferably not easily recognisable, as a toddler for example!

Instructions for visual aids, or stage directions are in italics within the talk. If possible, begin with a blackout of lights.

Before there was even any light, God decided to make the world. It was... well it wasn't really anything, and even if there'd been any people there to see, they couldn't have seen anything, because it was dark.

And God said 'Let there be light...' O right... *(lights on)* ... now we can see. But there still wasn't much to see and there weren't any people there to see anything yet anyway.

God made some more stuff. He made so much stuff I get muddled up about what order he made them in... and I don't think I've got my pictures in the right order anyway. Can you help? *(Add in day and night, sky and earth, land and sea, plants and trees, fish and birds, animals and people. Make sure there's plenty of repetition and ham up getting the pictures muddled as much as you feel comfortable with.)*

I'm still not sure we've got it in the right order but we'll play a game in a minute to get that right. Whenever God had made something, it says in the Bible that he looked at it and said, 'That's good!' And when he finished making it all he said, 'That's very good!!' And then he had a rest.

Oh, there's one picture we've not seen yet. *(Look at the acetate.)* It's something God said was very good. It's really special because when he made this, God said, 'I'm going to make someone a bit like I am myself.' Wow! Here it is! *(Show the acetate of yourself. Assist them, if they need it, in recognising you, comment how you've lost weight, got much more hair etc. Emphasise that you're not being vain.)* God made people in his image as the special part of creation, to be like him – free, able to love, to do what's right. So I could have put a picture of any of us there and said, 'Here's someone really special that God made.'

You recognised me because even though I've changed a lot/bit I'm still the same person. Being made to be like God doesn't mean we look like him. It's to do with what we're like inside, how we think and know what's right and wrong, how we can make and imagine new things, how we can love and be loved. But right from the beginning people weren't very good at staying much like God. We all do too much that's wrong, and it's quite hard to see what God's like by looking at most people and what they're like. So God had a plan to put all that right. That's what **MegaQuest** is all about – God's plan to put the whole universe he made, right again. And the plan was that there would be one man who was perfect, so that we really can see in him what God is like. But before Jesus came there were some other levels in the plan. I wonder what tomorrow's will be...

Anyway, we'd better get back to the Garden Level where we are today and make sure we've really understood what God did when he made everything: *(Encourage them to call out all of the things God made.)* And what did he say when he'd made them? ... It was very good! And what did he say when he made you?...

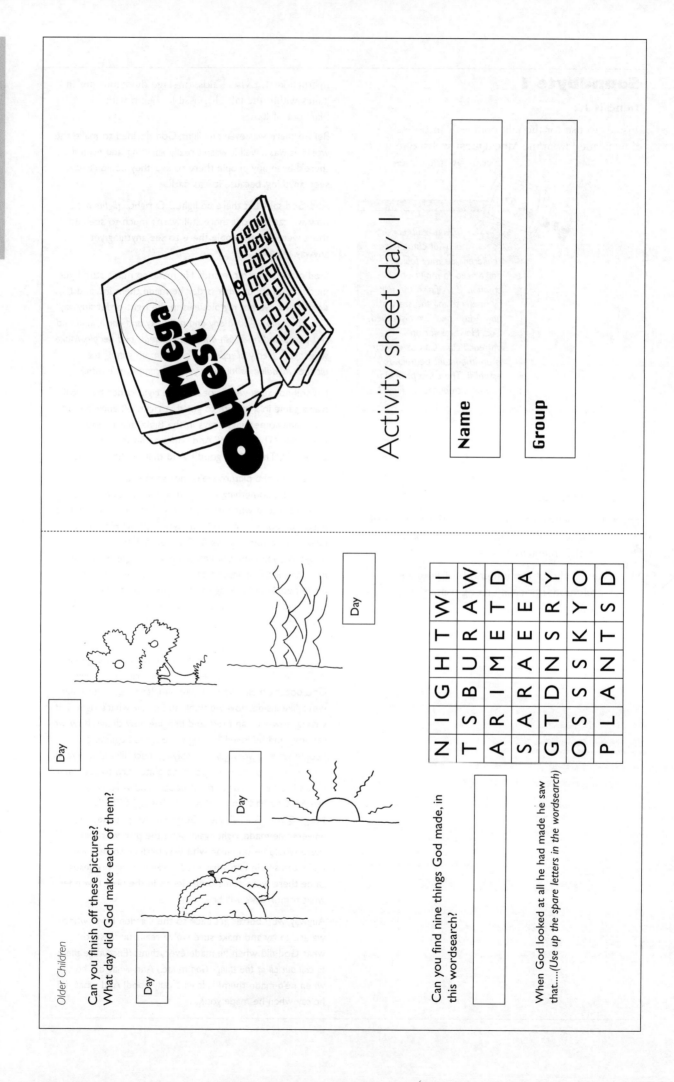

MegaQuest

Activity sheet day 1

Name

Group

Older Children

Can you finish off these pictures?
What day did God make each of them?

Day

Day

Day

Day

Can you find nine things God made, in this wordsearch?

N	I	G	H	T	W	I
T	S	B	U	R	A	W
A	R	I	M	E	T	D
S	A	R	A	E	E	A
G	T	D	N	S	R	Y
O	S	S	K	Y	O
P	L	A	N	T	S	D

When God looked at all he had made he saw that..... (Use up the spare letters in the wordsearch)

Younger Children

Put these pictures in the order that God made them. Join each thing to the day at the side.

Day 1

Day 2

Day 3

Day 4

Day 5

Day 6

Day 7

Can you finish the other half?

Picture to colour

Talk with God

Thankyou for all you have made. Thank you

especially for...

And thank you that you made me. Amen

Level 2:
The mountain

Aim

To explore the fact that God's plan was to remedy the badness in his spoilt world. He gives the ten commandments on Mount Sinai to show how people should live in a way that pleases him. But even after that, mistakes are made and God is disobeyed.

Bible Base: Exodus 19,20, 32–34; Galatians 3: 15–25

It is a vital stage in God's plan that he communicates how people should live in his world. He does this by choosing a group of people to belong to him, revealing to them what he is like, rescuing them, making a covenant with them and laying down his standards for them. But it is not just for them. He wants all nations to share in this.

We concentrate on the law in today's teaching. But we aren't to imagine that God's intention was that giving the law would do the trick. Nor that the people's disobedience and our disobedience took him by surprise. Just as creation looks like something that went wrong, so too the giving of the law looks like a Plan B that fails too. But God never imagined that the people who said, 'We will do everything the Lord has commanded', would actually do it! Galatians 3:15-25 helps us to understand the place the law has in preparing the way for Jesus.

Some of us perhaps managed to grow up misunderstanding Christianity as a religion of law-keeping in order to keep God sweet. Many outside the church will have that misunderstanding too. We may bend over backwards so much in trying to avoid that idea, that we shy away from teaching how God wants us to live. In Deuteronomy 6:20-25 we read how the great stories of God as a rescuer are to be told to the children when they ask 'Why did the Lord give us these laws and teaching?' We'll look together at how God wants people to live in his world, recognise we can't do it and be ready for the next level in his BIG plan.

You will need

- Video episode 2 or visuals for Soundbyte 2 which can be downloaded from the **MegaQuest** website.

- OHP pictures of well-known people.

- Card jigsaws for the Interactivity **Can you recognise them?** – one for each group.

- Plaster tablets, templates, pencils and nails for craft activity **Tablets of Stone**.

- Activity sheet 2 and pencils/felt-tips.

- Screen picture 2.

Welcome

Group leaders encourage involvement in continuing the model computers. The screen should have been made so that a picture related to today's story can be attached to it. (For a screen picture use the picture on the activity sheet for Day 2.) Encourage the children to talk about themselves and what happened yesterday. Some children may have brought in a completed activity sheet.

On-line in the Upload Zone

According to how you have set up the Mountain Level, exaggerate the need for care as you enter the zone. The children could pretend to get puffed and you may like to 'rope' them together as if climbing a mountain.

Talk a bit about the level, and establish the fact that you are up a mountain!

Sing

Sing the first verse of the theme song, emphasising that **MegaQuest** is about God's BIG plan. Today we will learn about the next level in it.

The Interactivity:

Can you recognise them? (a group-based quiz)

Use the Interactivity to chat about being made in God's image and how it is spoilt by the wrong things in the world.

This is a two-part game following up the idea of being made in God's image, but introducing the idea of that image being spoilt.

Part one

Display on the OHP a series of photos of well-known people (ranging from the Queen to Tinky-Winky and from Tony Blair to Zoe Ball). There should be some easy and some hard, preferably all likely to be known by some within the age-range. After each one is shown, gather the range of verbal suggestions, one from each group, and give the answer and award points. An alternative would be to disguise the photos in some way (for example with glasses or a moustache before copying them). After six or seven, announce that the final round is a bit different and will be worth enough points to allow all teams still to have a chance of winning!

Part two

Prepare enough copies of a jigsaw for all the teams. Photocopy a photo of a well-known person onto card and cut into a ten piece jigsaw using straight lines. All jigsaws must be identical!

Put each set into an envelope, retaining the piece which contains the face. Give each group an envelope and announce that the points will go to the team which first assembles the jigsaw and tells you who it is. After a couple of minutes, if no one has complained, you may need to prompt them to see if they have a problem. Admit you spoilt each jigsaw by taking a piece out. How difficult it is to recognise someone's image when it's spoilt! Then get one person from each team to come and get the missing piece, then race to complete it and shout out who it is. In the chaos announce a draw, unless there is a clear winner!

Post it

> "One way to make identical jigsaws is to copy a picture, cut it up, reassemble on the copier and copy the rest.
>
> Then cut along the visible lines on the copies."

Pogo challenge

Video/Soundbyte

Use the **MegaQuest** video, episode 2, or use Soundbyte outline 2 on page 41.

Groups

Aim:

- To chat further about the way God wants us to live in his world and how difficult we all find it.

Spend time doing the activity sheet which contains a number of items to follow up this discussion.

Refreshment break

Games

As appropriate and if time.

Craft

Tablets of Stone

You will need:

- Plaster tablets. These can be made using finishing plaster (25kg sack costs about £3).
- Plastic ice-cream tubs (you will need loads of these so it's an idea to start collecting weeks before the holiday club).
- Nails (4" will do nicely), one per child.
- Templates of a suitable commandment text for younger groups. For example, 'Love the Lord your God', 'Worship no God but me', or a selection of (short) commandments.
- Sandpaper for removing pencil marks and small mistakes.
- Felt-tips, pencil crayons or paint.

Method

Beforehand

Make one tablet per child. Mix up sufficient plaster to half fill all the tubs you have. It should be thick (as if you were about to use it for real on a wall). Use a trowel or another tool to fill moulds to the depth required. (It is easier if you have cut down the tubs

to a little taller than the depth you require.) Shake and tap the moulds to cause the plaster to 'flow' level and remove air bubbles. Leave for an hour or two to set, turn out and repeat until you have enough. 25kg of plaster will make more than 50 and this number would take someone about 3 hours in total to make, spread over a day or two, using ten tubs at a time. They can be done well in advance, but 'engraving' them will be easier and less dusty if they are still slightly wet.

On the day

Each child engraves a suitable text using the nail. Use pencil (and template or stencil for younger children) and then scratch deeply and repeatedly. Children will need to be encouraged to keep going to get a really effective look. Encourage decoration around the text. The words can be brought out more distinctly, either by colouring into the scratched-out letters, or shading over the whole surface without getting colour into the letters, or doing both in contrasting colours.

Back in the Upload Zone

This second time together will include the second episode of *The Virus Buster* and the song below which picks up the theme. You may have time for another Pogo Challenge and, if it seems appropriate, a short prayer, saying sorry for the things we do wrong.

Make sure you teach the bridge section of the theme song, and go back to the first verse to complete the tune.

10 commandments song for Day 2 (Copyright unknown. To the tune of *This old man...*)

This song is great fun and surprisingly easy for children to learn.

Post it

At the times when you pray explain briefly what you're doing, and that Amen means 'I agree'. So we shouldn't say it if we don't agree, or if we haven't been listening because we won't know what we're agreeing to!

Chorus	Number *one* out of ten, God gave
rules	for women and men...
Verse I	Do not worship anyone but me I alone your God will be
Chorus	Number *two* out of ten, God gave rules for women and men...

Verse 2   Don't make idols, images to praise
         What you make can't take my place

Chorus etc

Verse 3   Keep my name a special one
         I am God the holy one

Verse 4   One day a week you must keep free
         Save that day to worship me

Verse 5   Show respect, love your mum and dad
         This will really make God glad

Verse 6   Do not murder anyone or kill
         That would be against my will

Verse 7   Live your lives without adultery
         That sin breaks up families

Verse 8   Do not steal and take what isn't yours
         Pay attention to my laws

Verse 9   Never lie or say what isn't true
         I am God. I care for you!

Verse 10   Don't be greedy, wanting all you see
         Show content, not jealousy

Soundbyte 2

Exodus 19, 20, 32–34

Instructions for the speaker are in italics.

Arrange for a sound effect of lightning and thunder to be available. If using a CD, the track can be set to repeat indefinitely and can be faded up and down as needed. A loud trumpet blast is also needed – maybe a compressed air foghorn. If you have acquired a smoke machine for the beginning atmospherics, have extra smoke at the right point in the re-telling.

Briefly talk about creation at the first stage in **MegaQuest.** *Explain about God's relationship with his special chosen people, from Abraham, Joseph, the slaves in Egypt and the rescue from Egypt. Re-tell the arrival at Sinai, and Moses up the mountain.* They'd been walking through the desert for weeks and weeks, hot and dusty.... And then they stopped. These were God's special people through whom he'd chosen to show the whole world how he wanted people to live in his world. Moses their leader went up the mountain, because God had things to tell him to tell all the people.

Encourage the children to participate by repeating what the people say.

'We will do everything the Lord has commanded' *(Exodus 19:8).*

With plenty of sound effects paint a verbal picture of Moses going up the mountain to hear what God was going to say (Exodus 19).

The people wanted to hear what God had said... 'We will do everything the Lord has commanded.'

And God said... *(If you think the children you have will know something of the ten commandments, use your bad memory as an excuse to get them to help you recall them. In* **MegaQuest,** *an attempt has been made to phrase the ten commandments in a modern child-friendly way. You will find this version on the activity sheet for Day 2. The wording in the song is slightly different to fit the metre of the tune and to make a rhyming couplet. Each time you list a commandment, the children cry out*

'We will do everything the Lord has commanded.'

And that's not all he said. God told Moses loads of stuff about how he wanted his people to live in his world. But those ten things were the most important. And remember the people had all said... *(children repeat 'We will do...')* That's a really good thing to say – but only if you do what you say!

Moses went up the mountain again but this time he was up on the mountain for ages and ages and ages and ages and the people got fed up with waiting. They didn't even wait to hear what God had said, so they could do it. They got hold of Aaron, Moses' brother, and told him to make them a god. What a stupid thing to do, to replace the God who had made everything with some tinny little statue who hadn't made anything at all. In fact, the people had had to make him themselves! And what was the first commandment God had said? *(Encourage children to tell you.)* ...And what had the people said? *(They repeat the Israelites' response.)* ...And no sooner had God said it than they'd done just what he said they shouldn't.

If this won't take you over the concentration time of the children, tell them about Moses coming down, the broken tablets, the new ones etc.

And ever since, it's been the same. Even when we know what God wants, we find it really hard to do it. Even when we say we will do everything the Lord says, we often do just what we shouldn't. God knew it would be like that. It was part of his BIG plan to make sure that people knew how God wanted them to live in his world. But he knew they couldn't do it and he knows we can't do it either.

That's why there are more levels to **MegaQuest,** and on one of them God himself does something really special not just to show us how he wants us to live, but to rescue us from the mess we get ourselves into. He will forgive us for what we do wrong. But today we're still on the Mountain Level, so we'd better make sure we know the really important things God said in this part of his plan about how he wants people to live in the world he made.

Activity sheet day 2

Name

Group

Older Children

What should you do? Put a tick by the right things and a cross by the wrong ones.

Be friendly?

Be selfish?

Give to charity?

Be kind?

Share things?

Help others?

Steal?

Throw stones?

A B D E G H I K M N O P R S U Y W

Can you work out one of God's laws with the code bar?

Younger Children

Which way did Moses climb the mountain?

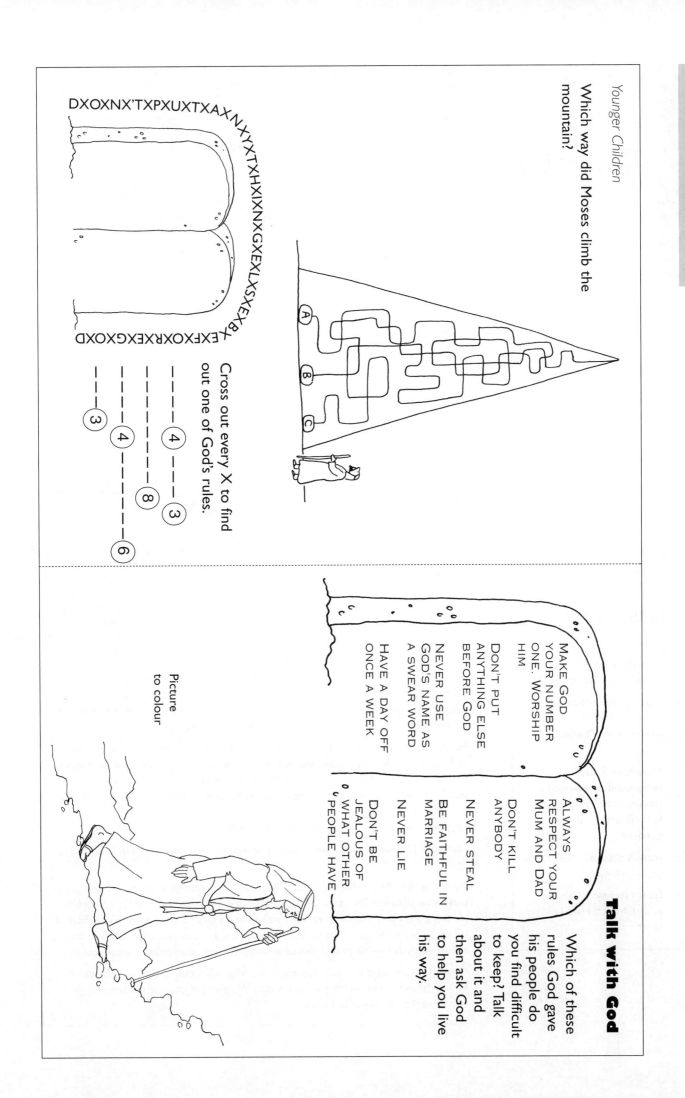

DXOXNX'TXPXUXTXAXNXYXTXHXIXNXGXEXLXSXEXBX
EXFXOXRXEXGXOXD

Cross out every X to find out one of God's rules.

— — — — ④ — — — ③
— — — — — ④
— — — — — ⑧ — — ③
— — — — — — ⑥

Picture to colour

MAKE GOD YOUR NUMBER ONE. WORSHIP HIM

DON'T PUT ANYTHING ELSE BEFORE GOD

NEVER USE GOD'S NAME AS A SWEAR WORD

HAVE A DAY OFF ONCE A WEEK

ALWAYS RESPECT YOUR MUM AND DAD

DON'T KILL ANYBODY

NEVER STEAL

BE FAITHFUL IN MARRIAGE

NEVER LIE

DON'T BE JEALOUS OF WHAT OTHER PEOPLE HAVE

Talk with God

Which of these rules God gave his people do you find difficult to keep? Talk about it and then ask God to help you live his way.

Level 3:
The hill

To focus upon Jesus, who in God's BIG plan puts right the relationship between God and his world by his self-sacrifice. There is nothing more that anyone needs to do – except accept God's plan.

Post it

In this programme we have placed the teaching input into the second half, bringing the drama forward. This is partly to separate the quiz, (which has quite a lot of content), from the video/talk. It also demonstrates that the programme can be structured differently to suit your needs. You know what suits your group best!

You will need

- **MegaQuest** video, episode 3 or visuals for Soundbyte 3.

- Quiz scoring system and questions for the Interactivity: **The Jesus quiz.**

- Yoghurt pots, tomb backgrounds, seeds, tape, colours, compost for gardens for craft activity **Easter gardens.**

- Activity sheet 3, pencils/felt-tips

- Screen picture 3. Use the picture from the activity sheet.

Bible Base: Matthew 27; Mark 15; Luke 23; John 19; Romans 5: 1–11

Take time to reflect on the cross. It can be very tempting to rush and try to explain the mechanism of atonement. There are biblical pictures to help us understand – the courtroom (we are acquitted, although guilty, because Jesus paid our penalty), the slave-market (we are redeemed, bought back by Jesus our kinsman/friend); the battlefield (Jesus the victor has defeated sin and death); the temple (Jesus the perfect blood-sacrifice).

But these are difficult for children to grasp. The situations are not familiar ones to assist understanding, but rather, are ones which can confuse. Very often the Bible itself simply declares the effectiveness of what Jesus did, rather than trying to explain it. Jesus' own words were accompanied by a painfully explicit action as he broke the loaf and poured out the wine:
'My body... my blood... for you' (Matthew 26:26–28).

Romans 5:10: 'Even when we were God's enemies, he made peace with us, because his Son died for us...'

But we need to be careful. The cross only makes sense coming at the end of the perfect life Jesus led. This stage of God's plan is the one mega-event of his incarnation, life, dying and rising. We try to reflect that by using a quiz to recap some of the facts of his life before we focus on the cross. And even though tomorrow looks firmly at the resurrection, that needs to be referred to today. For no resurrection = no gospel.

Once again, this stage of God's plan looks like failure. But this, as God himself suffers for our failures, is the central part of the plan. Wonder and pray for the awe and glory of it to register in hearts and souls.

Welcome

Children arrive, are registered and are welcomed into groups. Lively music (band or tape/CD) should be playing. Group leaders encourage involvement in continuing the model computers.

On-line in the Upload Zone

Try to ensure that the sombre atmosphere of looking at the crosses comes over as you encourage the children to speculate about the level. There is a delicate balance to be found – keeping plenty of fun running through, while being really serious (but not heavy) about Jesus' death.

Sing

Sing the theme song so far, emphasising that **MegaQuest** is about God's BIG Plan. Today we will learn about the next level.

Pogo challenge

The Interactivity

The Jesus quiz.

(Emphasise the care, goodness and authority of Jesus as shown by the answers.)

Using whatever scoring method you've chosen, set up a quiz between groups, with this basic question: Can you tell me something you know that Jesus said or did? This is intended to allow you to provide a basic understanding of the sort of life Jesus led up to his death, which is the day's theme. Fill out the answers with brief explanatory comments. If you don't feel comfortable with such a totally open-ended approach, then prepare questions.

If you use the quiz computer you will need to ask more conventional, prepared questions with a multi-choice answer. For example:

1. Jesus once fed 5000 people by a lake. Did he

a) dial-a-Palestinian-Pizza?

b) get everyone to share their lunch?

c) pray over a boy's packed lunch, and then make it enough to go round?

2. Jesus once fed a group of people with 5 loaves and 2 fish. How many people were there?

a) 5 people.

b) Just 500 boys and girls.

c) More than 5000 people.

Use the answers to underline Jesus' perfect life, but also the growing opposition to him.

Quiz Advice

You may want to use a quiz each day or at any other family event or service. For ideas read the **Quiz Resource Book** Richard Chewter (SU) (see inside cover for details). Here are a few ideas to get you started.

1. A large game of pairs with, say, six types of fruit hidden under the numbers 1-12 will give scope for the right length of quiz. A child who gives a correct answer, chooses two numbers. If they find a pair, they keep it and score one point for their team. If not, the fruits are covered up again and the next question is asked.

2. Use a set of the cards you have prepared for Creation Swaps (Day 1 Interactivities, page 33) for the same kind of game. The idea would be to find the other half of the pair, for example, fish/bird or land/sea.

3. Build a 'computer' using the diagram below. It has three buttons to press (as a multi-choice quiz), with the correct choice giving a green light and bell, the two wrong ones a red light and buzzer. (The hidden three-way switch enables you to set which button will light up the green light without the children seeing.)

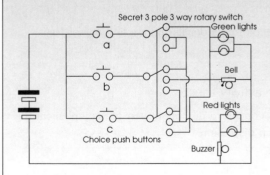

(Design: Steve Hutchinson)]

Drama

The third episode of *The Virus Buster*.

Games

As appropriate and if you have time.

Refreshment break

Back in the Upload Zone

Video/Soundbyte

Use Episode 3 of the **MegaQuest** video or use Soundbyte outline 3 on page 47. You might want to learn the second verse of the theme song here, or leave it until the closing all-together slot.

Group

Aim:

To explore the details and implications of Jesus' death.

The activity sheet

This contains a number of items to complement the group discussion.

Craft:

Yoghurt pot Easter gardens

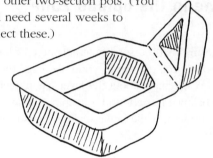

You will need:

- 'Crunch-corner' type yoghurt pots (where fruit/topping and yogurt are in separate sections of the pot.) The artwork on page 19 is designed to fit only these. It would need to be modified if you use other two-section pots. (You will need several weeks to collect these.)

- Artwork on page 19 copied onto card for each child.
- Tape.
- Compost (Compost 5 litres is fine for about 50 children).
- Seeds (fast growing, reliably germinating, ie cress).
- Colouring pens.
- Scissors.

Method

Each child colours the background artwork and cuts down the dotted line carefully. Fold up the corner of the pot and insert it through the cut-out. Tape the card around the main pot. Cut out and stick the card stone across the 'tomb'. Fill the pot with compost and sow the seeds.

Back in the Upload Zone

This third all-together time will include a song which picks up the theme, maybe another Pogo Challenge and, if it seems appropriate, a short prayer saying thank you to Jesus for dying for us. You will need to hint at the resurrection.

Soundbyte 3

Matthew 27; John 19

Instructions to guide the speaker are in italics.

Think of using effects such as arranging for the lighting to be dimmed suddenly as you tell of the darkness while Jesus was on the cross.

Pick up from the earlier quiz the sort of things Jesus did. Depending on the time of year, use Christmas to hook into the reality of his birth and his family. Emphasise the perfectly good life he lived. Then say...

But sadly people aren't good (and that's all of us really) and we don't like goodness. It shows us up. Jesus had enemies who didn't like him, because of what he did and it came to the point where they decided to get rid of him...

Concentrate on telling dramatically and accurately the story of the betrayal, trial, whipping and killing of Jesus. Don't side-step the details, but be sensitive in not dwelling on the physical violence. Pray for the right balance. Use children's experience of being let down by friends, lied about or hurt, as entry points into what Jesus did for us. If the dynamics allow for it, respond to questions.

Careful thought is needed about the level of explanation to give. The Bible is often content to say simply that it was for us, for forgiveness. Assert it positively. It's the heart of God's BIG plan, and the deepest revelation in his heart and character that he gives us.

Jesus used the picture of a seed dying in order to bear fruit (John 12:24) Explain this, and take the opportunity to point forward to the resurrection, of which we'll find out more on the next level. This links into the craft activity which involves seeds.

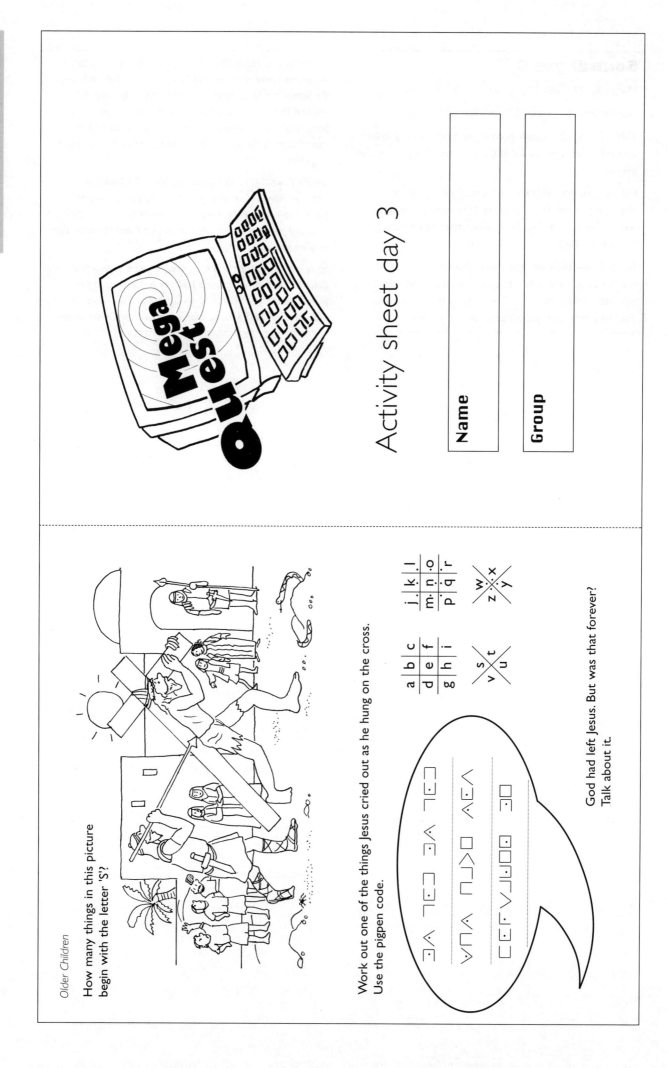

Activity sheet day 3

Name

Group

Older Children

How many things in this picture begin with the letter 'S'?

Work out one of the things Jesus cried out as he hung on the cross. Use the pigpen code.

a	b	c
d	e	f
g	h	i

j	k	l
m	n	o
p	q	r

God had left Jesus. But was that forever? Talk about it.

Younger Children

Spot the eight differences between these pictures

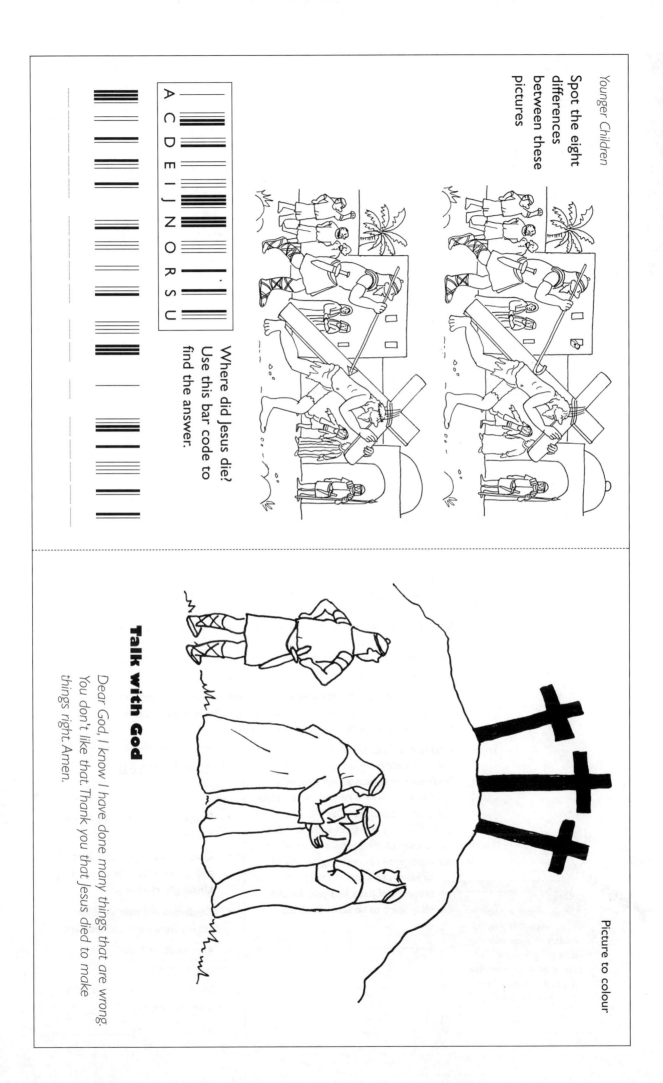

A C D E I J N O R S U

Where did Jesus die?
Use this bar code to find the answer.

Picture to colour

Talk with God

Dear God, I know I have done many things that are wrong. You don't like that. Thank you that Jesus died to make things right. Amen.

Level 4
The road

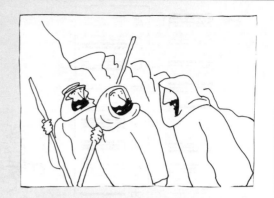

Aim

*To concentrate on the fact that death
was not the end for Jesus.
He came alive and still lives.
He is with us and we can know him.*

Bible Base: Luke 24:13–49

We focus on the two disciples going home. They had thought that something special was happening in God's plan. But now there were some strange rumours, odd loose ends, a missing body – but nothing more. However, God has a surprise for them, as they come to know for themselves the truth of the resurrection. For them it was as their hearts were warmed on the road and as the penny finally dropped at the meal-table. We don't know why they didn't recognise him at first.

But then we don't really know why our spiritual eyes opened when they did, when the truth 'dawned' on us. It certainly wasn't because we'd reached a certain age, or were clever enough to work it out.

Jesus said to Nicodemus, 'You must be born from above before you can see God's kingdom.' John 3:3. It's the Holy Spirit, blowing where he wills, who warms hearts and opens eyes. Day 4 is where God's BIG plan interfaces with our lives. As we learn of the Emmaus two and share our experience of coming (gradually or suddenly) to know the truth and presence of Jesus, let's pray for the Holy Spirit to be active in all our lives.

Post it

There will be an opportunity for group leaders to share how they came to understand that Jesus is alive for them. Spend time in preparation talking about how you will do this.

You will need

- **MegaQuest** video, episode 4 or music and lighting for Soundbyte 4.

- Quiz scoring system (see page 45) and questions for the Interactivity **Untangle challenge**.

- Cardboard and nails for craft activity **Sunrise scraperboard**.

- Activity sheet 4 and pencils/felt-tips

- Screen picture 4 for the activity sheet for Day 4.

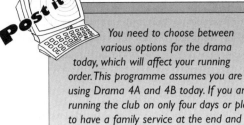

Welcome

Children arrive, are registered and are welcomed into groups. Have lively music (band or tape/CD) playing. Remind the children that tomorrow the computers will be judged, with a prize for the best. You may want a prize for different age groups.

On-line in the Upload Zone

Speculate with the children about the sun on the wall. Is it rising or setting? Perhaps we'll find out later.

Sing

Sing the theme song so far emphasising that **MegaQuest** is about God's BIG Plan. Today we will learn about the next level.

The Interactivity

Untangle challenge

Groups stand in a circle and take hands with the two people either side of them. Children step over or under each other's arms without letting go. On the word 'go',

each group must untangle itself back into a circle again without letting go of either hand. With a large number of children, you may want to do this with several circles of children who are the same age.

Pogo challenge

Drama:

Episode 4A of *The Virus Buster.*

Refreshment break

Games

As appropriate and if time.

Back into the Upload Zone

Video/Soundbyte

Use the **MegaQuest** video, episode 4 or use Soundbyte outline 4 on page 53. You might want to learn the second verse of the theme song here, or leave it until the closing all-together slot.

Group

Aim:

To chat further about how anyone can come to know the truth of Jesus' living presence. See talk outline for more details. This is an opportunity for group leaders to talk about their own experience of God.

Activity sheet:

These contain a number of items to follow up this discussion.

Craft

Sunrise scraperboard

You will need

- Thick card – enough for one piece per child. (It is easier to make the board in large pieces and guillotine it to size. It needs to have a matt surface.)
- Wax crayons in sunrise colours.
- Nails (as for day 2).
- Black paint (made up with water and detergent).

Method

Beforehand:

Cover the card with strips of crayoned wax colours in reds, oranges and yellows. Paint over the colours with the black paint and leave to dry. Cut to size.

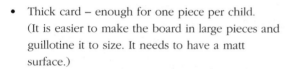

Post it

If the card is too shiny the wax will scrape off too. If you only have shiny card, omit the colouring of the card. Just paint black paint on the card to make a monochrome 'scraperboard' and provide bright felt-tips for the children to use on the 'bare' parts of their finished pictures if they wish.

On the day:

Children scrape a sunrise picture with the nail. The point can be used for outlining, and the round end, or the edge of the pointed end, for 'shading'. Ensure that not too much of the scraped off black paint ends up on clothes!

Alternative suggestion.

Let the children make their own scraperboard by colouring the whole piece of card in sunrise colours themselves. Then cover it all with a dark colour crayon. Finally scrape to make a picture as above.

Back into the Upload Zone

This third time all-together time will include a song which picks up the theme, another Pogo Challenge and, if it seems appropriate, a short prayer saying thank you that Jesus is alive and here with us now.

Drama

Episode 4B of *The Virus Buster*.

You may want to begin advertising any special events that follow up **MegaQuest**, like a special service on Sunday or other activities – see page 62 for ideas.

Soundbyte 4

Luke 24:13–49

Instructions to the speaker are given in italics.

Describe in as graphic language as possible, the picture of the sad friends who think it's all over as they set out to walk home. Have a bird song sound effect ready for the appropriate time, and arrange to have lighting faded down. We're not yet sure whether the level is sunset or sunrise...

They'd thought that something really special was happening. Jesus was the one they'd been waiting for, the one who'd put God's big plan into action. But then they'd seen him die... They'd seen him buried and all the loose ends tied up so they were going home. The sun was going down as they left Jerusalem.

It felt like that in their hearts too. All the hope was fading away. It was all over.... And so they were walking home. Not just 5 minutes walk though. They lived 11 km away. That's about as far as from here to *(name a place 11 km or so from where you are)*! Have you ever walked that far? Think how tired you'd be! And they didn't have the option of buses or cars or trains!

As they were walking, someone joined them. Someone they didn't recognise. Later they would ask themselves why they didn't recognise him. Was it too dark? Did they need glasses? Come to think of it, they didn't have those then either!

Anyway, as they walked they talked. And the stranger asked why they were so sad. And they told him. *(Repeat yourself a bit!)* And then he told them they were daft – that it had to be like that! That it said so in loads of places in the Bible. That God's special person had to die to make God's plan work. And that it wouldn't be the end, because he'd come back, even though it seems impossible...

And they felt oddly warm inside as they listened, and excited and tired too, I bet. By the time they arrived home it was really late, and even though the stranger looked as though he wanted to go further, they persuaded him to stay.

So they set about getting something to eat. They'd been away a while. In those days they didn't have fridges and freezers or microwaves. What did they have available which hadn't gone mouldy or rotten? There's always bread and that keeps quite well. Or maybe they'd been to the baker on their way home. Anyway, they had some bread.

The stranger picked up the loaf and said grace. He broke it into pieces. And then, suddenly, they realised who it was. It was Jesus! He was alive! He was with them! They recognised him! It was all true! Hadn't they felt it when he was talking to them? Then suddenly he'd gone – disappeared. They didn't know where. But they knew where *they* were going. Right back to Jerusalem to tell the others! Yes, not just as far as, *(name a place 4 km from you)* but the distance of going there and all the way back too. Maybe the sun was coming back up again by the time they got there. And on the way back they knew it wasn't the end (like a sunset is the end of a day), but the beginning (like a sunrise is the beginning of a new day), of something new and better, as God's BIG plan moved on to a new level.

And people ever since have found the same thing ... maybe on a road, over a meal, or at a club like **MegaQuest**.... Old people, young people... *(You may be able to give a brief testimony yourself, especially if you can refer to when you were a child, and/or mention someone known to you who firmly recalls an awakening to faith as a child)...* even the leaders here at **MegaQuest**. And now you're going to have a chance in your groups to ask your leader to tell you how they came to realise Jesus is alive for us today...

This needs to have been thought through with the leaders beforehand. Ensure that each group has at least one leader willing to share in this way, without embarrassing any helpers.

- *Don't be tempted to duck this one! Sharing our experience of the reality of Jesus' presence is a vital part of evangelism.*

- *Don't give a long, prepared testimony. Answer the children's questions simply and honestly.*

Activity sheet day 4

Name

Group

Older Children

You can find all these answers in Luke 24:1-35

Across

1. The disciple who ran to the tomb
6. Where Jesus was buried
7. They discovered Jesus was - - - in the tomb
9. We celebrate that Jesus is alive at E - - - - -
13. Where Jesus first taught his disciples
14. The two friends first met Jesus on the - - - - -

Down

2. Where the two friends lived
3. How Peter got to the tomb
4. It was - - - - - so the friends asked Jesus to stay
5. This was rolled away
8. Peter did not - - - Jesus in the tomb
10. Who said Jesus was alive?
11. The friends rushed back to Jerusalem to - - - - - what they'd discovered
12. Jesus broke this

Colour in the shapes with a dot to find out something amazing!

Younger Children

How many people were walking together on the road out of Jerusalem? Join up the dots to see.

Cleopas and his friend rushed back to Jerusalem. They wanted to tell what they had found out. Can you help them find their way?

Picture to colour

Talk with God

Jesus is alive today. That means we can know him and talk with him. That also means he can be with us at/in .... and .... and ....Thank Jesus that he is with you in these places and at these times.

The Final Level
The city

Aim

To explore what heaven will be like – a new creation where there will be no more pain or tears – something to look forward to. This is the culmination of God's plan.

Bible Base: Revelation 21, 22

The Bible doesn't answer many of the questions everyone, including children, asks about heaven. If we can avoid speculating about pets, football, harps versus guitars or anything else and concentrate on the vivid pictures of these chapters, we can focus on what it seems that God wants us to know. The bejewelled city of gold – translucent in its purity and redolent with the symbols of completeness and perfection – grabs the imagination, even if the mind struggles to grasp it. And Eden redeemed and restored, with the tree and flowing river of life reminds us that God's plan began and will end just as he intended it, right at the beginning.

Revelation 21:4 is a key verse. No more of anything that spoils, that saddens or that clouds. We can all think of our own particular sadnesses which we never want to know or experience again. Some children will already have known deep sadness, others won't yet. But among the more uncomfortable promises of the Bible are the words of Jesus in John 16:33: 'While you are in the world, you will have to suffer...'. We are brought back to the darkness-shattering words that marked the first act of God's BIG plan, by these words of completeness in Revelation 22:5: 'There will be no more night. The Lord will give them light.'

These words naturally lead to words of invitation: 'Do you want to be there?' Or as Revelation 22:17 has it: 'If you are thirsty, come. If you want life-giving water, come and take it. It's free!' Let's be faithful and urgent in extending that invitation, and let's pray for a heart-felt response of willing acceptance of all that God offers.

You will need

- **MegaQuest** video, episode 5 or picture for Soundbyte 5.
- Large cards for Interactivity Part 1, **Postcards from heaven.**
- Octons for Interactivity Part 2, see page 57.
- Artwork from page 20 and 21, copied onto tracing paper; colours.
- Activity sheet 5 and pencils/felt-tips
- Screen picture 5 (You will need to take one from the website or design your own, since there isn't a picture on the activity sheet for Day 5. However you may not need one since you will be finishing off your computers and maybe going round to admire each others!)

Welcome

Children will be comfortable in what has become familiar surroundings, but some may be sad that this is the last day. Group leaders encourage involvement in completing the model computers. Before going 'on-line', and in a way that is manageable with your numbers of children, get everyone to look at other group's computers. Announce the winner later (perhaps at the end, or just before the refreshments) so the winning group can share the prize!

On-line in the Upload Zone

Encourage speculation about the level, and if/when they guess, point out that no matter how hard you tried you couldn't possibly have made anything as good as God has in store at the end of his BIG plan.

Sing

Sing the theme song so far, emphasising that **MegaQuest** is about God's BIG plan. Today we will learn about the last level, which is still in the future – something for us to look forward to.

Pogo challenge

Drama

The final part of *The Virus Buster*.

As this is the last episode of *The Virus Buster*, make sure you thank the actors at the end. If you are keeping the finale for a family event or service, make it clear what is happening (and promise you'll tell what happens to anyone who really can't be there!)

The Interactivity Part 1

Postcard from Heaven

Give each group a large card and invite them, as a group, to imagine writing a postcard from heaven. Group leaders should not offer correction here. Use it as a chance for the children to bring out their assumptions and ideas. It should be a light-hearted exercise!

Call them together to find out a bit about what the Bible says heaven is like. (Collect up the cards, and if funny and/or appropriate read them out later.)

Video/Soundbyte

MegaQuest video, episode 5 followed by Interactivity Part 2, or use Soundbyte outline 5, first part on page 59.

Interactivity Part 2

Octons

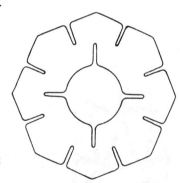

You will need a plastic constructional set of octagonal translucent plastic pieces. The original trade-name is 'octons', but a set is also available from Early Learning Centres as 'Constructons'. You need at least one octon per child.

Give out a number of octons to each group as they sit still in the Upload Zone. Get them to build a structure. With a smallish club, these can then be joined to one another. With a bigger club, have the structures brought to the front and left by the OHP.

Place the structure on the deck of the unlit OHP, with the mirror closed so that it won't project when switched on. Dim the lights if you can. Comment on the colours and shape. Then, without initial comment, turn on the OHP to illuminate them from below. Wait for the 'wow'.

Soundbyte part 2

Refreshment break

Games

As appropriate and if time.

Group

Craft
Stained glass pictures

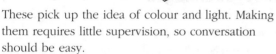

These pick up the idea of colour and light. Making them requires little supervision, so conversation should be easy.

You will need:

- Artwork from page 20 and 21, photocopied onto A4 tracing paper.
- Bright felt-tips

Method

Children either colour in the picture or the shapes on the shield. You could make card frames for the pictures. At home they can fix it to a window.

Alternative suggestion

I Glass marbling

If your budget and your facilities stretch to it, try marbling glass as you would paper, using glass paints, or glass painting. Designs could be ready-drawn for younger children using the outlining material, so that only the coloured areas need to be filled. You could paint a small glass or jar and place a short broad candle or night-light inside.

2 Wire dipping

Use liquid plastic that dries translucent over a wire frame like a bubble film.

3 Candle-making

This picks up both the light and colour images of heaven.

Activity sheets

These pick up the theme of heaven and provide further opportunity for conversation. In particular, they develop the idea of postcards from heaven.

Back into the Upload Zone

This second all-together time will include part 2 of the talk as appropriate, maybe another Pogo Challenge and the time to complete the song with the last verse and closing shout. The closing announcements should include an encouragement to come to the weekend event(s) and a really warm goodbye to those who won't be able to be there. (Don't make them feel bad about it!) Mention your regular activities and follow-up plans and have ready details about the family event(s) to give to parents. Leave time for...

Final group time

This needs to include good-byes. Try to ensure it isn't rushed.

Post it

None of these is a cheap option unfortunately. Good art/craft shops will advise (and happily take your money).

Soundbyte 5

Revelation 21,22

Heaven

Instructions to the speaker are in italics.

The Bible material in Revelation 21 and 22 is not really narrative, which makes story-telling difficult. Moreover, the pictures are figurative (e.g. transparent gold) and attempts to illustrate run the risk of reducing the awe-inspiring nature of these images. It is suggested that you may use the artwork made available on the MegaQuest web-site, showing the pictures of a golden city, a river and a tree while describing what the Bible says. The main visual element requires the use of a plastic constructional set of octagonal translucent plastic pieces called 'Octons'.

Soundbyte Part 1

Begin by reminding the children about the BIG plan so far. Emphasise that God always had the end in mind, the perfect end far better than we could ever dream of. Although there's loads and loads we don't know about heaven/the end, the Bible does tell us about a vision that someone called John saw, which helped him help us to know about it.

Describe the city of gold (and if you use a picture, comment how much better the vision was than any picture you could find). Do the same for the 'garden' images of tree and river.

But the best thing is the light. Do you remember the first thing God made?...

Recap the light/dark themes throughout the Bible material we've covered.

There's always a mix isn't there? And darkness is a nuisance, even if you're not frightened of it.

Talk briefly about a power cut, especially if there has recently been one in your area. You could turn off the lights, and speak illuminated by just a lamp or candle.

But the Bible says that in heaven at the end of God's BIG plan, there'll be no lamps, no sun even, because it'll be full of the light of God himself, so great and so bright that there'll be no darkness at all!

If you've dimmed the lights, then they should come on at the right point. Garden flood lights can be cheaply bought and two or three make for a very bright contrast to the darkness.

And we're going to do something together which shows what a difference light can make.

Interactivity Part 2

Octons

Comment on the amazing transformation the light brings and talk again about the picture of heaven flooded with the light of God's presence. Show each structure in turn if there are several, or add them to one another. It is possible to project the structure onto the screen and use the focus adjuster to focus on different levels. At the same time talk briefly about how all the jewels and other pictures in Revelation promise a huge variety in the perfection of what God has planned when he makes everything new at the end of his plan.

Soundbyte Part 2

Read, with great animation the words from Revelation 21:4. Add, for example, no more school, no more tests. Stop to make it clear that you've added those, but that it's OK because that is what that verse means - no more of anything that spoils life. Not a mix of light and darkness, just light. Is it too good to be true?

If you can, tell of an offer that sounded too good to be true. Suppose you didn't take it up, yet subsequently found it had been genuine. Or you still don't know if it's true but wonder if it might have been genuine.

Some things are a con but some things really are too good to miss. And heaven is one of those. So how can we be sure of not missing out?

Well heaven is the end of God's BIG plan for all those who've got to know Jesus, accepted his friendship and been forgiven... It's an offer we don't have to collect coupons for, or send off a form. We can say 'yes' any time and we need to go on saying 'yes' as we learn more of God's plan.

There is going to be an opportunity for children to say 'yes' if they want - maybe for the first time, maybe the 29th time - to God who made us all and knows us all and loves us all.

He hears not just what we say, but what we think..

One possibility is to invite all the children to clasp both hands into fists, and if they really want to say 'yes' as you've described, to squeeze one hand.

No one else will see or know, but God knows. He promises to say 'yes' to everyone who says 'yes' to him.

Suggest, with no great fuss, that in the group time, they may want to chat about what you've just been saying.

60

Older Children

Can you match up these questions with the right answer?

Has anyone come back from heaven?

Is there room for me?

In heaven, will my body be old and worn out if I'm old when I die?

I do wrong things sometimes. Will God let me in?

Jesus has promised there's room for all who trust him.

No. Everyone in heaven has a new body that is perfect. It will never wear out.

We all do wrong things. Jesus died so we could be forgiven. ALL his friends will be in heaven.

Only Jesus. And it's only because of him that we can get there anyway.

Talk together about this. Then thank God that Jesus will be in heaven, waiting for us.

Can you find all these words about heaven in the wordsearch?

Brilliant
Wonderful
Peaceful
Eternal
Better
Happy
Light
Home
Jewels
Life

Throne
Joy
God
Jesus

T	X	P	B	H	A	P	P	Y
N	X	E	E	S	J	E	X	H
A	J	A	T	L	O	T	T	O
I	E	C	T	E	Y	E	H	M
L	S	E	E	W	X	R	R	E
L	U	F	R	E	D	N	O	W
I	S	U	X	J	X	A	N	X
R	X	L	I	F	E	L	E	X
B	L	I	G	H	T	G	O	D

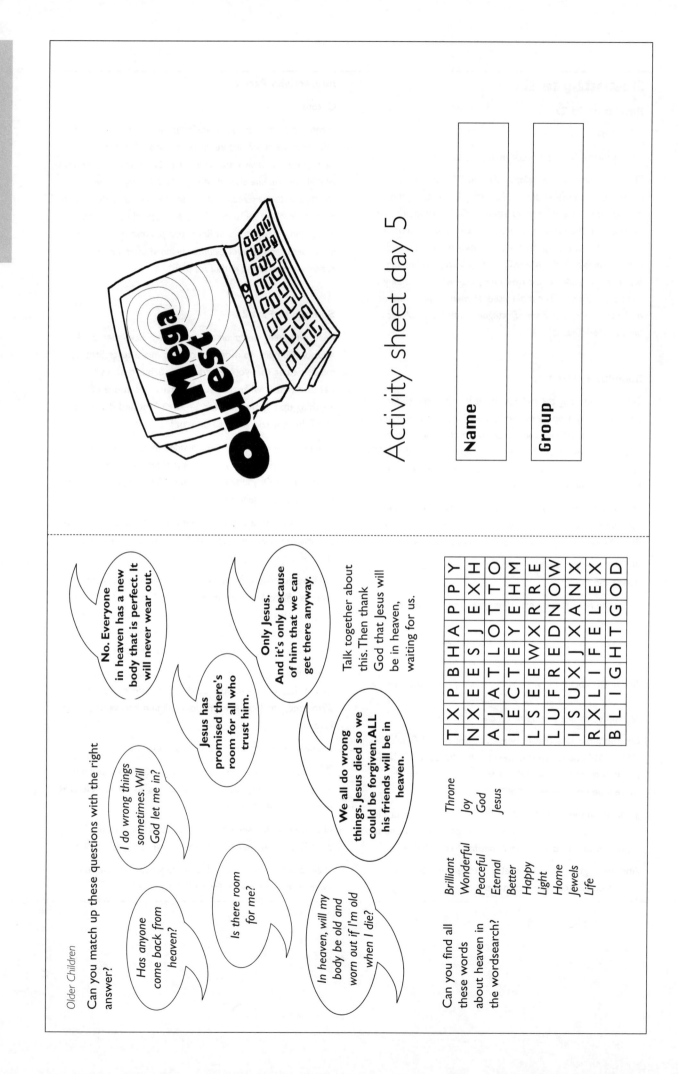

Activity sheet day 5

Name

Group

Younger Children

John saw lots of jewels in heaven. Heaven is full of light and beauty. Colour these jewels in the right colour. (You may need some help!)

◇ Diamond

◯ Ruby

⬭ Emerald

▭ Amethyst

Colour in the letters and draw your face in the O. This is what Jesus said to his friends. He was talking about heaven.

I am going there to prepare a place for each one of yOu.

Dear ....

Heaven is brilliant. There are no .... or .... but it is never .... Heaven is full of God's light.

To ....

....

....

....

In the space, write what else you think John might have said.

After MegaQuest

Plan to put together an event or two, to which you can invite all of the children and their families. It could be an evening towards the end of the week, or Saturday afternoon, or a Sunday all-age service. Plan to build bridges not just to the children but their families too. Remember, Sunday services can present a big barrier to non-church attenders, so think about the following issues:

1 If you want to encourage children into your regular Sunday groups

Choose Sunday for the first follow-up event, but make sure everyone feels welcomed. Plan the **MegaQuest** programme so that Sunday morning is advertised as the final club time, with part of the time as the 'normal' Sunday programme and the rest as the last **MegaQuest** time. Encourage the regular children's leaders to be there as well as the club leaders so that they can get to know the children. Invite parents to come and make it clear they'll have a choice of coming out with the children or staying in for the rest of the service. Knowing there's an 'out' half way through, will make some more willing to give it a try.

2 If your main follow-up will be a weekday club or invitation events

Put your main efforts into a non-Sunday event. Use a closing service to celebrate the week and share it with the congregation. Be ready to welcome newcomers and plan for the future with them in mind. Make sure the team members are there to provide continuity for non-church children.

3 For an evening or Saturday event

Choose a time which will be most convenient for those who are coming. What else is happening at the same time in your locality?

- At the appropriate times in the following year have a barbecue or special party (for example, an alternative Hallowe'en or Christmas event). Or just have an all-age fun time, with different games for all-age groups.

- You could try a reunion day and use video and photos taken during the **MegaQuest** week. For a fun evening, keep it short and light and make sure the clear Bible truths you mention come over as information to the adults of what's been happening in the club. That way no-one will feel preached at. But the truth can still be communicated.

- It may be appropriate to offer an invitation to a 'Just Looking' or Alpha course if parents want to find out about God's BIG plan which has been the focus of the holiday club week. Parenting courses have also proved to be a valuable way of building on contacts with families of holiday club children.

4 Is a personal visit possible?

If all your leaders are willing and able, it is not too much of a task to visit all the children who came to **MegaQuest**. Such a visit can make contact with families and inform them of your regular activities. Also you can gather useful information (perhaps via a questionnaire) about the shape of future events that would appeal to the families visited.

What's on the MegaQuest website?

http://www.scripture.org.uk/megaquest

We hope to have a number of useful resources on the **MegaQuest** website which will include at least the following:

Resource materials for download

1 Some coloured artwork from the video to be used as pictures for the talks or for the junk model computer screens. (NB. They are used with the permission of the artist Colin Smithson and are not to be reproduced in any form for financial gain.)

2 5 pieces of b/w artwork from the video to be used as a picture to go on each computer screen.

3 Copy of the drama script to be adapted by users for the needs of their group. There is also a summary of the plot to facilitate the adaptation (see page 23-31 of this book).

4 Updates (suggestions/material not available at the time of going to print).

5 Training case studies for preparing the team.

6 The music for the song and a recording of it (page 13 of this book).

Extra information

1 Creating the right environment (an expansion of pages 14–16 of this book).

2 Using a computer, overhead projector and video (page 16,17 of this book).

Feedback from users

1 Bulletin board/newsgroup for sharing ideas and experiences with other **MegaQuest** users.

Material for children

1 Email letter box to link with other groups using material during the club.

2 Email questions box answered by SU.

CRWI/
RWC

Order Form

To order any of the resources recommended in this book from Mail Order, complete this form.
The books should also be available from a local Christian bookshop.

ISBN	TITLE	QUANTITY	PRICE (each)	PRICE (total)

	TOTAL COST OF GOODS	
	Postage & Packing	
	Donation to Scripture Union	
	TOTAL ENCLOSED	

When ordering, please include ISBN, title, quantity and price.
All titles subject to availability.
Prices subject to change without notice.

Ordering Information

Please complete the payment details below.
All orders must be accompanied by the appropriate payment.
Send this completed form to:
Scripture Union Mail Order
PO Box 764,
Oxford, OX4 5FJ
Tel: 01865 716880 Fax: 01865 715152

Postage and Packing Rates

Order Value	UK	Europe	Rest of World Surface	Airmail
£6.00 & under	£1.25	£2.25	£2.25	£3.50
£6.01-14.99	£3.00	£3.50	£4.50	£6.00
£15.00-29.99	£4.00	£5.50	£7.50	£11.00
£30.00 & over	FREE	PRICE ON REQUEST		

Ordered by

Mrs/Mr/Miss/Ms/Revd _____

Address _____

_____

_____

Postcode _____

Daytime tel _____

(for any query about your order)

Delivery address (if different)

Mrs/Mr/Miss/Ms/Revd _____

Address _____

_____

_____

Postcode _____

Daytime tel _____

(for any query about your order)

Payment Details

Method of Payment: ☐ Cheque*   ☐ Mastercard   ☐ Visa   ☐ Switch   ☐ Postal order*

Credit card number: ☐☐☐☐ ☐☐☐☐ ☐☐☐☐ ☐☐☐☐   Expiry Date: ☐☐☐☐

Switch card number: ☐☐☐☐☐☐☐☐☐☐☐☐☐☐☐☐   Expiry Date: ☐☐☐☐

Issue number of Switch card: ☐☐☐☐

Signature: _____   Date: _____

(necessary if payment by credit card)

*made payable to Scripture Union

Please print name which appears on credit card: _____

Please print the address the card is billed to, if different from above: _____